KNOTS IN AUNTY'S ROPE

Karen "Zow" Kolzow

Copyright © 2023 by Karen "Zow" Kolzow
All rights reserved. No part of this book may be used or reproduced in any form whatsoever without written permission, except in the case of brief quotations in critical articles or reviews.
Printed in the United States of America.

For more information or to book an event, contact: zowproductions@yahoo.com
Book and cover design by Karen "Zow" Kolzow
Prepared by Ready Writer Publications, LLC
ISBN - Hardcover: 978-1-961668-00-3
ISBN - Paperback: 978-1-961668-01-0
First Edition: May 2023

Unless otherwise noted, all scripture is taken from the New King James Version, copyright 2018 by Thomas Nelson and used by permission. All rights reserved.

Quotes have been either author-referenced or remain unknown.
All efforts were made to identify un-referenced quotes.
"Shared by" quotes are the source by whom they were received.

Oh, my Tikvah,

*Being found by YOU
humbles me into
a rightness of receiving
all I could desire
and nothing I deserve.
It was,
and is,
and always will be...
YOU!
You are my home!
There are no words
but THANK YOU!
You didn't change my life,
You became it.*

THREADED THIS WAY

	INTRODUCTION	5
1.	NOT A KNOT *About God*	13
2.	TAUT-TAUT *Truth*	23
3.	KNOT ALONE *Me and God*	35
4.	GOD, I'M IN KNOTS! *Upsets*	49
5.	ANCHORED IN *Faith*	57
6.	TUG OF WAR *Before the Prize*	69
7.	TIGHTENING THE KNOTS *Common Sense*	81
8.	ROPE BURN *Told You So's*	93
9.	A BRAIDED LIFE - *True Disciple*	105
10.	LEARN THE ROPES *Talents*	119
11.	STRONG STRANDS *Strong Stands*	129
12.	TIE THAT BINDS *Love Wins*	139
13.	TIED THE KNOT *Marriage*	149
14.	TENSILE STRENGTH *Relationships*	159
15.	HANG LOOSE *Other Aware*	171
16.	KNOT-A-FRAYED *Leadership*	181
17.	KNOTS OF OLD *Elders*	193
18.	END OF THE ROPE *Next Stop, Eternity!*	201
	HONORING MY STRONG THREADS	212

The storms of life are inevitable. They are often filled with raging waves and unpredictable forecasts, leaving us tossed around, unmoored, and off course. But what if someone who had made it to shore tossed you a knotted rope, pulled you to dry land, and helped you stand on your feet again? Eventually, your sea legs would strengthen, and the rope would find a new purpose; to hold down, pull forth, or help you climb to greater heights.

Open these pages and get roped in...

WHY KNOTS?

The completion of *Knots in Aunty's Rope* just missed my eldest nephew's graduation by sixteen years. In fact, it missed ALL my niece's and nephews' graduations! Had it made the mark, I would have scribbled a little note in the front of their books saying something like this …

Dearest Kyle, Shanni, Michael, Joeli, and Luke…

I want to extend a part of myself by entrusting to you
these nuggets of truth God has so generously shared with me.
They are windows into my soul…
a view into my own vulnerabilities and character weaknesses,
each of which has required me to take hold of a knot in the rope of truth,
…knots in a rope that would keep me climbing,
stay me from falling,
and secure my footing.

Grasping these knots has steadied me on the precipice of life
as I have swayed back and forth between my own inconsistencies.
These are rough jots extrapolated from my journals over recent years.

Here's to you, dearhearts!
I toss the rope…
With oodles of love!

Your Aunty!

THE LIFE OF A ROPE

If you're like me, you acquire a rope with a particular use in mind. After that, it goes on a hook or in a bin in the garage…

…Until opportunity presents!

The camp-out needs a clothesline.
The neighbor kid borrows it to tow his friend on a skateboard.
The garage sale needs an area roped off.
A stray beagle needs to be secured.
The orange tree is leaning too far to the right.
Your kid cuts it in half, "so both of us can jump rope."
Life happens!!
…A rope is needed.
Life throws challenges!!
…Truth is needed.

I NEEDED A ROPE

I never intended to collect quotes. *Knots in Aunty's Rope* was an organic assemblage of truths intertwined in my faith journey that eventually came in handy for others, too.

My primal quest was understanding how faith works: How do I go from reading about the woman who got healed to being healed myself? How do I read about a life radically transformed to being transformed myself? How do I know a historical Jesus as He was, the Ancient of Days, in my modern mayhem?

For years, my wonder wrestled. Could He really love me if He knew me? Could He possibly forgive me and remember my sins no more? Could He powerfully use me? That was my impossible dream. I had religion, but I needed Him!

I saw Jesus Christ on the pages but not in my stages. On October 27, 1990, I decided to lay everything down. If I lost it all, I deemed Him worth it! I wanted to know Him at all costs.

Astoundingly, the very next day, I lost the thing that mattered most to me. I was utterly broken and angry. My choice was to go bitter and die or to go through and cry! It was life or death. I was willing to die to know Him.

IT WORKED FOR ME!

He pulled me in. He tied me down. He taught me the ropes!

Through years of grief-filled tears and desperate prayers, the Holy Spirit led me with much scriptural counsel. I journaled and jotted as He taught me to hear and obey His voice. Jesus was making me into His very own disciple, the one I always wanted to be! In comparison, my old life began to look and smell like a corpse.

Using vulnerability with Spirit-led mentors and godly friendships, the Holy Spirit showed me how to use the rope you will soon read about. Being rescued from tumultuous dark waters was just the beginning. I eventually learned to rappel off life-threatening cliffs of disappointments and offenses. God used this rope of hope to adventure me into realms my natural life could never know.

PERHAPS YOUR LIFE NEEDS SUCH A ROPE

When we get to the end of our rope, one way or the other, we find He was there all along. The gift of needing a rope is that on this side of eternal life, we have the privilege of being drawn by God into the adventures of His heart. It is by being with Him that we are taught the ropes of His Kingdom. To know Him is to love Him. To be known by Him is…

Abundant life, with joy!

Aunty Zow

Quotes for Growth

"Whoever ponders is sure to wander in paths the wonder goes ~"

Zowie

> *Light needs no introduction and requires no explanation.*
>
> *Zow*

1
NOT A KNOT

About God

All that I am is for You, and all that I have for You is all that I am.
God to Zow

*BEHOLD, GOD IS MIGHTY, BUT DESPISES NO ONE.
HE IS MIGHTY IN STRENGTH OF UNDERSTANDING.
Job 36:5*

*BUT THE WORD OF GOD IS NOT CHAINED.
2 Timothy 2:9b*

Christ went more willingly to the cross than we do to the throne of grace.
Thomas Watson

Creation cost Him nothing; salvation cost Him everything.
Reinhard Bonnke

Even after all this time, the sun never says to the earth, you owe me!
Look what happens with a love like that! It lights up the whole sky.
Hafiz

Extravagance!

*FEAR NOT, LITTLE FLOCK, FOR IT IS YOUR FATHER'S
GOOD PLEASURE TO GIVE YOU THE KINGDOM.
Luke 12:32 KJV*

God does little with much; He does much with little;
and He does everything with nothing.

God has a way of giving by the cartloads to those who give away by the shovelfuls.
Charles Spurgeon

God has no problems, only plans.
Corrie Ten Boom

God hates disease as much as He hates sin.

God uses the least amount of pressure to produce the most amount of change.

God wants to, and will, if we call upon His Name!

God whispers to us in our pleasures, speaks in our consciences,
but shouts to us in our pain.
C.S. Lewis

God will take from you what no one else wants and
give you what others would die to have.

God's vulnerability cries out to us, and He waits to be wanted.
A.W. Tozer

*HE IS ALSO ABLE TO SAVE TO THE UTTERMOST
THOSE WHO COME TO GOD THROUGH HIM.*
Hebrews 7:25

*...HE STANDS AT THE RIGHT HAND OF THE NEEDY,
TO SAVE HIM FROM THOSE WHO JUDGE HIS SOUL.*
Psalm 109:31 NASB

HIM THAT LOVETH VIOLENCE HIS SOUL HATETH.
Psalm 11:5b KJV

*HOW BLESSED IS THE ONE WHOM YOU CHOOSE AND
BRING NEAR TO YOU TO DWELL IN YOUR COURTS.*
Psalm 65:4 NASB

How did Christ learn obedience? –Through suffering. *(see Hebrews 5:8)*

I did not love her because it was "right", I just loved her.
Horse Whisperer

I will make lovers of God, My warriors,
and warriors My heroes.
God to Zow

If there is no God, all is permitted.
Fyodor Dostoevsky

If you want to make God laugh, tell Him your plans.

IN ALL THINGS GOD WORKS TOGETHER FOR THE GOOD OF THOSE WHO LOVE HIM, WHO HAVE BEEN CALLED ACCORDING TO HIS PURPOSE.
Romans 8:28 NIV

In God's economy, nothing is wasted.
Schatzie

It is not prayer that fetched the deliverance but mercy that sent it.
Matthew Henry

Jesus' blood deals with what I have done. His cross deals with what I am.

Justice ensures we receive all the benefits of heaven. The cross of Jesus is God's justice!
John Paul Jackson

Light needs no introduction and requires no explanation!
Zow

Love depends on the One loving, not the one receiving.
Zow

Masses are seeking signs; true seekers will find My presence.
God to Zow

My grace will decide for God's glory.

...NOT THAT WE LOVED GOD, BUT THAT HE LOVED US
AND SENT HIS SON AS AN ATONING SACRIFICE FOR OUR SINS.
1 John 4:10 BSB

Perfect and true are all His ways Whom heaven adores, and earth obeys.
Annie C. Lee Monument Inscription

RIGHTEOUSNESS WILL GO BEFORE HIM,
AND SHALL MAKE HIS FOOTSTEPS OUR PATHWAY.
Psalm 85:13

THE EYES OF THE LORD ARE IN EVERY PLACE,
KEEPING WATCH ON THE EVIL AND THE GOOD.
Proverbs 15:3

The greatest miracle that God can do today is to take an unholy man
out of an unholy world and make him holy,
then put him back into that unholy world,
and keep him holy in it.
Leonard Ravenhill

The Lord may not fulfill our concepts of what we think He should do,
but He will always accomplish His Word.

*THE SACRIFICES OF GOD ARE A BROKEN SPIRIT, A BROKEN AND
A CONTRITE HEART - THESE, OH GOD, YOU WILL NOT DESPISE.*
Psalm 51:17

The same sun that melts the ice hardens the clay.
Vance Varner

The timing of God is eloquence.
Zow

*WE KNOW THAT GOD DOES NOT HEAR SINNERS,
BUT IF ANYONE IS GOD-FEARING AND DOES HIS WILL, HE HEARS HIM.*
John 9:31 BLB

We may not feel secure in what God is doing,
but we can always be assured of Who He is.

What is it you seek?
If you do not know, you are a wanderer.
Seeking to find requires intentionality.
God to Zow

...'*WHATEVER YOU DID FOR ONE OF THE LEAST*
OF THESE BROTHERS AND SISTERS OF MINE,
YOU DID FOR ME.'
Matthew 25:40b NIV

WHOEVER DOES NOT LOVE
DOES NOT KNOW GOD, FOR GOD IS LOVE.
1 John 4:8 BSB

YOUR THRONE, O GOD, IS FOREVER AND EVER;
A SCEPTER OF RIGHTEOUSNESS IS THE SCEPTER OF YOUR
KINGDOM. YOU LOVE RIGHTEOUSNESS AND HATE WICKEDNESS...
Psalm 45:6-7a

YOUR WORD IS TRUTH.
John 17:17b

Wow!

Love cannot penetrate what truth does not facilitate.

Zow

2
TAUT TAUT

Truth

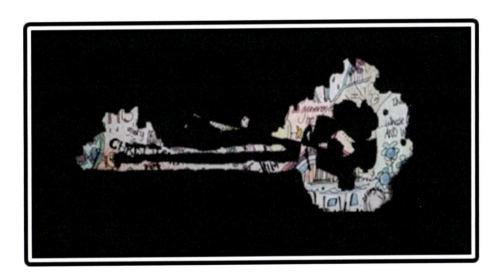

A drop of honey gathers more flies than a gallon of gall.
Abraham Lincoln

A Greek definition of truth: Having nothing concealed.

A little knowledge with an overabundance of zeal always tends to be harmful.
Involving religious truths, it can be disastrous.
Kathryn Kuhlman

A portion of truth distorts the truth.
We are commissioned to preach all the truth.
Baruch Korman

A sight of Christ's death, if it is a true sight, is the death of sin.
Charles Spurgeon, The Bitterness of the Cross

A sin nature will not go away without a sin remedy.

A truth uttered before its time is always dangerous.
Mencius

A watered-down gospel is no gospel at all.
David Wilkerson

After all, what is a lie? 'Tis, but the truth in masquerade.
Lord Byron

ALL SCRIPTURE IS GIVEN BY INSPIRATION OF GOD, AND IS
PROFITABLE FOR DOCTRINE, FOR REPROOF, FOR CORRECTION,
FOR INSTRUCTION, FOR INSTRUCTION IN RIGHTEOUSNESS.
2 Timothy 3:16 KJV

Always make a practice of provoking your own mind to think of what it accepts easily.
Our position is not ours until we make it ours by suffering.
Oswald Chambers

Ask "why" of the Holy Spirit when reading God's Word.
"Why" is the spiritual metal detector that locates unearthed wisdom
which remains safely hidden from the intellect.
Zow

Cut the Bible anywhere and it bleeds.
William Evans

Death is much sweeter to me with the testimony of truth than life with the least denial.
St. Angelo, Italian Martyr

Difference of opinion leads to inquiry and inquiry leads to truth.
Thomas Jefferson

TAUT-TAUT - *Truth*

Does darkness come in or does light get shut out?
Zow

DOES NOT THE EAR TEST WORDS AS THE PALATE TASTES FOOD?
Job 12:11 ESV

Every truth we truly believe, we live by!
That is why we are known by our fruit, not our words.

...EVERYONE WHO IS OF THE TRUTH HEARS MY VOICE.
John 18:37

Facts and truth are not the same.

Grace gives me the ability to do what truth demands.

He that complies against his will is of the same opinion still.
Samuel Butler, 1684

HE WILL USE EVERY KIND OF EVIL DECEPTION
TO FOOL THOSE ON THEIR WAY TO DESTRUCTION,
BECAUSE THEY REFUSE TO LOVE AND ACCEPT
THE TRUTH THAT WOULD SAVE THEM.
2 Thessalonians 2:10 NLT

Hypocrisy is the compliment vice pays to virtue.
Shared by Nick Freitas

I am coming to realize that the only power Satan has over me is the power of suggestion.
Zow

I am not bound to win, but I am bound to be true.
I am not bound to succeed, but I am bound to live up to the light I have.
Abraham Lincoln

I must stand with anybody that stands right.
Abraham Lincoln

IF ANY HOUSEHOLD OR TOWN REFUSES TO WELCOME YOU OR RECEIVE YOUR MESSAGE, SHAKE ITS DUST FROM YOUR FEET AS YOU LEAVE.
Matthew 10:14 NLT

If your truth is your own, so are your delusions.
Zow

In Scripture, silver points to redemption to indicate the purpose of our nature– which is to reflect the One Who purchased us.

Is the question, "What is meaning" not answered by the ageless question, "What is truth?"
Zow

*IT IS THE GLORY OF GOD TO CONCEAL A MATTER,
BUT THE GLORY OF KINGS IS TO SEARCH OUT A MATTER.*
Proverbs 25:2

I've never tried to be controversial; the truth is controversial enough.
Keith Green

Lies fracture the soul.

Love cannot penetrate what truth does not facilitate.
Zow

Love is vulnerable, truth is not. May we never compromise charity when we stand for truth.

My heart is for the gospel because the gospel has been for me.

Never worry about who will be offended if you speak the truth.
Worry about who will be misled, deceived, and destroyed if you don't.

NEVERTHELESS, WE MUST LIVE UP TO WHAT WE HAVE ALREADY ATTAINED.
Philippians 3:16 BLB

No man indulges in error of judgment without sooner or later
tolerating an error in practice.
Charles Spurgeon

One lie is enough to question all truth.

One must handle and act upon the truth
to see what may be yet concealed from the understanding of it.

One's first reaction to truth is hatred.
Tertullian

Only words backed by action are words that stand in truth.

Scripture directs us not to change the world but to testify of another world.
Rolland Baker

*...SEARCHED THE SCRIPTURES DAILY TO FIND OUT
WHETHER THESE THINGS WERE SO.*
Acts 17:11b

Seek and find and realize that truth does not lie openly on the surface.
Clem H.

Sincere: To be without wax. What you appear to be is what you are.
Example: Potters would sometimes fill broken vessels with wax and paint over them to sell. Heat and wear would unveil the deceit and imperfections, revealing their "in"sincerity."

TAUT-TAUT - *Truth*

STAND BY THE ROADS, AND LOOK, AND ASK FOR THE ANCIENT PATHS,
WHERE THE GOOD WAY IS; AND WALK IN IT AND FIND REST
FOR YOUR SOULS. BUT THEY SAID, 'WE WILL NOT WALK IN IT'.
Jeremiah 6:16 ESV

Tell the truth.

The American gospel of the Kingdom has been
reduced to the gospel of salvation.

The author who benefits you most is not the one who tells you something
you did not know before but the one who gives expression to the truth
that has been dumbly struggling in you for utterance.
Oswald Chambers

The characteristic of counterfeit is not the opposite of truth.
The characteristic of counterfeit is that which closely resembles truth but is not.

The enemy attacks what it fears, not what it seeks to gain, though that would be the delusion.
Darkness does not have the power to gain more darkness.
Darkness only exists by keeping light from penetrating.
Its only way to advance is to seal off all light from its domain.
Light is powerful. Light is truth.
God to Zow

The essence of grace is supply. The essence of the law is demand.
Joseph Prince

The gospel's truth is my heart's marquee.
Zow

The nature of the gospel is eternal gladness; joy is most certainly its native tongue.
It is the glad message of the true, happy God.

The only people who are mad at you for speaking the truth are people who are living a lie.

The opposite of shame is intimacy.
Michele Wood

There is a principle which is a bar against all information,
which is proof against all argument,
and which cannot fail to keep man in everlasting ignorance.
That principle is condemnation before investigation.
Edmund Spenser

*THERE IS NONE WHO CALLS ON YOUR NAME,
WHO STIRS UP HIMSELF UP TO TAKE HOLD OF YOU.*
Isaiah 64:7a WEB

To enlist freedom, truth must be received, believed, and acted upon.

Truth and love are one reality!

TAUT–TAUT - *Truth*

Truth divides. Truth costs. Truth lives.
Zow

Truth doesn't hurt unless you're on the wrong side of it.

Truth often shines clearest when circumstances are the darkest.
Havalon Popous

Truth will ultimately prevail where there are pains to bring it to light.
George Washington

TRUTHFUL LIPS ENDURE FOREVER,
BUT A LYING TONGUE IS BUT FOR A MOMENT.
Proverbs 12:19 ESV

Ultimate truth never changes,
but our perception of that truth changes under daily observation.
Hollis Vaughn

We either believe the truth or we prove it.

That's solid!

> *He owes me nothing but gives me everything.*
>
> *Zow*

3
KNOT ALONE
Me and God

A single life is like a universe.

A turning point in our lives can be when we stop seeking
the god we want and start seeking the God Who is.

Alone time is when I distance myself from the voices of the world so I can hear my own.

Always ask questions of the Holy Spirit.
Zow

Beloved, I will hold out My promises to you at every turn.
God to Zow

Blessed is the mighty King who sits down beside the weakest man and
thinks of all their similarities.
Calvin Miller, The Singer

Boldness in requesting prayer displays faith in God's character.
God to Zow

Boxes unfolded are turned into crosses.

BUT HIS SECRET COUNSEL IS WITH THE UPRIGHT.
Proverbs 3:32

Choose your portion in the way that you seek.

Chronic lack of joy is a revelation of the absence of God encounters.
Bill Johnson

"Did you ever learn to love?" That is the question!

Do not accept the applause of men and you won't be destroyed by their criticism.
Reinhard Bonnke

Don't have faith in faith but have faith in God.

Eyes that look are common, but eyes that see are rare.
Kim Clemente

Every trial is designed for one purpose only which is to conform us into the image of Jesus.

Fantasy didn't create the universe.
Zow

Finish the race! Don't give up! Seek Me again and find Me. Don't seek only, but lay hold of Me. How I want to be sought! To be sought is a gift of longing, and longing is the seed of intimacy. Plant longing. Water it with your tears, and soon you will bear a crop of satisfaction.
Jesus to Zow

FOR MAN IS BORN FOR TROUBLE, AS SPARKS FLY UPWARD.
BUT AS FOR ME, I WOULD SEEK GOD AND I WOULD
PLACE MY CAUSE BEFORE GOD, WHO DOES GREAT AND
UNSEARCHABLE THINGS, WITHOUT NUMBER.
Job 5:7-9 NASB

FOR THE LORD TAKES PLEASURE IN HIS PEOPLE;
HE WILL BEAUTIFY THE MEEK WITH SALVATION.
Psalm 149:4 KJV

God is more interested in our desperate need for His lamp-lit direction than in our path-paving skills.
Shared by Ruth Chou Simons

GOD IS NOT UNJUST TO FORGET YOUR WORK AND
LABOR OF LOVE WHICH YOU HAVE SHOWN
TOWARD HIS NAME, IN THAT YOU HAVE MINISTERED
TO THE SAINTS, AND DO MINISTER.
Hebrews 6:10

God will remove your sin from you, or your sin will remove you from God.

God's promises are the invitation, not the guarantee.
Zow

Gratitude is the heart's memory.

He owes me nothing but gives me everything.
Zow

He that goes before the cloud of God's providence goes on a fool's errand.

He watches over the watch of those who watch the Lord.

Hope in God, not in determined outcomes.
Jack Deere

Humility and intimacy are keys to hearing God's voice.
Intimacy requires some secrecy on our part.
Go to your room, shut the door, and pray.

I did not give you a fate; I gave you a life!
God to Zow

I don't want to bring anything to Jesus that He doesn't bring to me.
Shelly England

I feel so ashamed in His presence, though He is so grand and noble.
He can hide my own defects from me better than I can myself.
Calvin Miller

I HAVE HEARD OF YOU BY THE HEARING OF THE EAR;
BUT NOW MY EYE SEES YOU. THEREFORE, I ABHOR MYSELF
AND REPENT IN DUST AND ASHES.
Job 42:5-6

I have tested you with many trials because you have asked for much.
It is in the asking that breaks open the testing which breaks
open the man to release his spirit.
God to Zow

I want to feel the beat of Your heart as it becomes my battle march.
Zow to God

I want to walk a life of "yes" and "Amen."
Zow to God

I will die living. I will not live to die.

If you are in the same place today as you were yesterday, you are a backslider.
Smith Wigglesworth

IF YOU ARE WILLING AND OBEDIENT, YOU SHALL EAT THE GOOD OF THE LAND.
Isaiah 1:19

If your encounters with God don't leave you with more questions
than when you started, you have had an inferior encounter.
Bill Johnson

Imagine God thinking about you! ABSOLUTELY imagine it!
Zow

In prayer, it is better to have a heart without words than words without heart.
John Bunyan

Is prayer your steering wheel or your spare tire?
Corrie Ten Boom

Je T'aime

Let Go! Let God! Let God Go!
Quote used by O. T. McRee

Love is so rich it borrows nothing and even repays evil with good.
Zow

MANY, O LORD MY GOD, ARE YOUR WONDERFUL WORKS
WHICH YOU HAVE DONE; AND YOUR THOUGHTS
TOWARD US CANNOT BE RECOUNTED TO YOU IN ORDER;
Psalm 40:5a

May I live as loud as I love you!
Zow

My intimacy with God intimidates the enemy.

One with God is a majority.
Schatzie

Opportunities of today are not those of tomorrow.
Do not live as though they may be repeated. Do not fail to enter every door,
nor be held back by feelings of unreadiness.
I AM your preparation.
God to Zow

Our Heavenly Father is the only one
Who can produce seed that is conceived in the human spirit.

Peace is joy resting. Joy is peace dancing.
Frederick Brotherton Meyer

Pray: The Hebrew root word means to judge or examine oneself.

Prayer is striking the winning blow; service is gathering up the results.
S. D. Gordon

Pride: Anything of my own initiative.

Prophetic people have a lifestyle of agreeing with God.

Quiplantavit Curabit: He who has planted will preserve.
Theodore Roosevelt

...REVERENT FEAR OF THE LORD
(WORSHIPING, OBEYING, SERVING, AND TRUSTING HIM WITH AWE-FILLED RESPECT)
PROLONGS ONE'S LIFE,
BUT THE YEARS OF THE WICKED WILL BE SHORTENED.
Proverbs 10:27 Amplified Bible

Stop asking God to bless what I'm doing and begin doing what God is blessing.

Thankfulness abounds in the culture of trust.
Thanklessness is the rottenness of fear, pride, and entitlement.
Zow

Thankfulness says, "I took You into my heart."
Appreciation says, "I took Your kindness into my use."
Zow

The affection of Jesus is the yearning cry of me.
Zow

THE LORD CONFIDES IN THOSE WHO FEAR HIM,
AND REVEALS HIS COVENANT TO THEM.
Psalm 25:14 BSB

The purposes of God rejected are the victories of God denied!

The sight of Jesus' death, if it is a true sight, is the death of all love of sin.
Charles Spurgeon

There is only one proof of the Holy Spirit in your life, and that is a holy life.
Leonard Ravenhill

THEREFORE, DO NOT WORRY ABOUT TOMORROW,
FOR TOMORROW WILL WORRY ABOUT ITS OWN THINGS.
SUFFICIENT FOR THE DAY IS ITS OWN TROUBLE.
Matthew 6:24

To hunger and thirst after righteousness is when nothing in the world
can fascinate us as much as being near God.
Smith Wigglesworth

True spirituality always neutralizes the flesh.
Graham Cooke

Until the soul quits asserting itself as boss,
one's spirit will be unable to commune with the Holy One
Who communicates Spirit to spirit.
Zow

We become like what we behold.

We have as much of God as our lifestyle requires. If we want more of God,
we must change our lifestyle so we would fail without Him.
Bill Johnson

We must give up all that we are in order to possess all that He is!
Heidi Baker

What are you going to do with a God like this?
What our Lord wants us to present to Him is not goodness nor honesty nor endeavor,
but rather real solid sin. That is all He can take from us.
And what does He give us in exchange for our sin? Real solid righteousness.
Oswald Chambers

What will it take for my gaze to desire only Him?
Zow

*WHATEVER YOU DO, WORK AT IT WITH YOUR WHOLE BEING,
FOR THE LORD, AND NOT FOR MEN,*
Colossians 3:23 BSB

When I fall, it's You Who sees, and You Who lifts me up.
When I see, I fall, and lift You up.
Zow

*WHO IS THIS THAT DARKENS COUNSEL
BY WORDS WITHOUT KNOWLEDGE?*
Job 38:2

You are a "peculiar and holy person".
You belong to God! Do not expect to fit into this world.
It is better to be right with God and
stand-alone than to be right with men and be against your God.
Schatzie

You are no slave to sin, no slave to man, and no slave to contrary opinions.
Do not revel in man's opinion of you or you will become like them,
taking in evil and fondling good. Both are corrupt.
Fire will test your works, whether they honor men or God.
God to Zow

You must make a demand upon Me!
God to Zow

He's IT!

> *When I wait upon God for His perspective, I can get through anything.*
>
> *Zow*

4
GOD, I'M IN KNOTS!
Upsets

Addictions promise joy but take everything from us.

An appeaser is one who feeds the crocodile hoping it will eat him last.
Winston Churchill

As a rule, man's a fool.
When it's hot, he wants it cool.
When it's cool, he wants it hot.
N'er contented with his lot.
Therefore, as a rule, man's a fool.
Opal Nedeleski

As believers, we do not fight for victory, but from victory.

Birds born in a cage think flying is an illness.
Alejandra Jodorowsky

Bitterness: Unfulfilled revenge.

Control: Something we fight to keep that we never really had.
Robin McMillan

Discontent is the first step in the progress of a man or a nation.
Oscar Wilde

Dying to myself includes dying to opinions of myself and relying on who God says I am. As I struggle to accept His report of me, I begin to live it.
Alan Smith

Entertainment promises worldly men renewal through external means; godly men are renewed by the Spirit of God within them.
Zow

Fallen man is not simply an imperfect creature who needs improvement, he is a rebel who must lay down his arms.
C. S. Lewis

False Guilt? How do you deal with it? Let it die.
Though you cannot stop its drumbeat, you can refuse to dance with it.
Wayne Jacobsen

Fear breeds deadening caution. Trust in God to lead me.

Fear travels in the vague, and faith travels in the specific.

For every action there is an equal and opposite reaction.
Sir Isaac Newton

God didn't purchase me as a chewy toy for Satan.
Zow

God has already condemned sin in me, so it has lost its power to condemn me.

He who proves himself receives the prize.

How would you treat a "friend" who lied to you as often as your fears do?
Jack Hayford

If a doctor has the last word over my life, Jesus is not my Alpha and Omega.
Zow

If forgiveness does not include action, there remains a legal right to accuse.

If we always did what was convenient, we would never do what was necessary.
Chris Newsome

If your life is broken when given to Jesus,
maybe it is because the pieces will feed a multitude.

Imagine God thinking about you. What do you assume He feels when you come to mind?
Zow

In the dry seasons, we are becoming the song.
Zow

It is not by the accumulation of evidence, but by My Spirit.
God to Zow

It is not what comes at you that matters, it's what comes out of you.
Graham Cooke

Men are not afraid of bondage but of freedom,
for in absolute freedom comes absolute responsibility to choose.

"No" is one of the most important words a Christian needs to learn if he is to stay on course.

Once you abolish God, the government becomes your god.
G. K. Chesterton

Perhaps I have an offense with God if I cannot rejoice in another man's breakthrough.

Strongholds are thoughts which -
... become considerations,
...which form attitudes,
... that manifest into actions,
... when repeated,
...form habits
... by which strongholds are built
...for the habitation of a spiritual being.
Zow

*THE GODLY MAY TRIP SEVEN TIMES, BUT THEY WILL GET UP AGAIN.
BUT ONE DISASTER IS ENOUGH TO OVERTHROW THE WICKED.*
Proverbs 24:16 NLT

The parts that hurt show us what is yet to die.
Zow

There is no pit so deep that God's love is not deeper still.
Corrie Ten Boom

Trials are for advancing faith, deepening love, and inviting great hope.

When I made the choice, I knew the cost.
I am willing to be alone on the ground of truth
than to be swayed by the millions of sheep being
pulled to the slaughterhouse.
Mosab Hassan Yousef

When I wait upon God for His perspective, I can get through anything.
Zow

When you find yourself in a hole, stop digging.
Rick Joyner

Help!

> *Faith enforces the promises of God.*
>
> *Zow*

5
ANCHORED IN
Faith

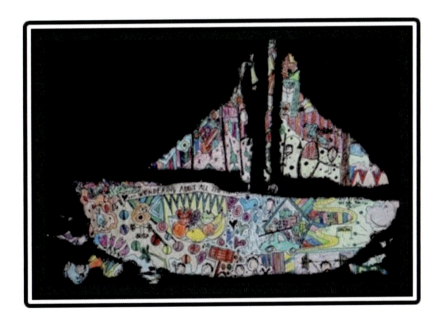

*AND IT CAME ABOUT, WHEN THE DAYS WERE APPROACHING
FOR HIS ASCENSION, THAT HE RESOLUTELY SET HIS
FACE TO GO TO JERUSALEM.*
Luke 9:51 NASB

*ANYONE WHO BELIEVES IN ME,
AS THE SCRIPTURE HAS SAID,
OUT OF HIS HEART WILL FLOW RIVERS OF LIVING WATER.*
John 7:38

Aren't you weary of talking about a gospel of power and seeing no demonstration of it?

*ASSUREDLY, I SAY TO YOU, WHOEVER DOES NOT RECEIVE THE KINGDOM OF GOD
AS A LITTLE CHILD WILL BY NO MEANS ENTER INTO IT.*
Mark 10:15

Be as a bird perched on a frail branch,
That she feels bending beneath her,
Still, she sings all the same,
Knowing she has wings.
Victor Hugo

...BE IT UNTO ME ACCORDING TO THY WORD.
Luke 1:38b

Because a thing seems difficult for you, do not think it is impossible.
Marcus Aurelius

BELIEVE IN THE LORD YOUR GOD,
AND YOU WILL BE ESTABLISHED;
BELIEVE HIS PROPHETS, AND YOU SHALL PROSPER.
2 Chronicles 20:20

Bloom: The time came when the risk it took to remain in the blossom
was more painful than the risk it took to bloom.
Anais Nin

"COME, FOLLOW ME," JESUS SAID,
"AND I WILL MAKE YOU FISHERS OF MEN."
Matthew 4:19 BSB

Credo Ut Intelligam: I believe in order that I may understand.
St. Augustine

Every piano key responds to its position and the touch of the musician's stroke;
its only response is to yield to his touch by going low.
Zow

Extreme purpose in God requires extreme obedience.

Faith believes in advance what only makes sense in retrospect.

Faith does not ignore reality. It does not call that which is as though it is not.
It calls that which is not as though it is.

Faith enacts what grace precedes.
Zow

Faith enforces the promises of God.
Zow

Faith holds an open hand to the Lord.
Zow

Faith: I believe what You say. Trust: I believe in Your character.

Faith is ignited by the Word of God and is fanned by His goodness.

Faith is in the nature of God; it is not faith in faith. Some say they do not have enough faith. The real issue is not the size of one's faith but rather the depth of revelation of God's nature.
Graham Cooke

Faith is spelled RISK.

Faith: Leaning the entire personality on God in absolute trust and confidence.

Faith propped up by external means either dissipates or is maintained
by self-righteousness, which ultimately props up pride.
Zow

Faith requires action.

Fear entertained is faith contaminated; fear contained is faith obliterated.
Zow

Fear is faith for the things you don't want.

Fear Less.   *Hope More.*   Talk Less.   *Say More.*

Fear looks. Faith jumps.

Fear of man is the greatest destroyer of faith.

God does not call the qualified; He qualifies the called.

God dwells in you, but you cannot have this divine power until
you live and walk in the Holy Ghost,
until the power of the new life is greater than the old life.
Smith Wigglesworth

HE IS ABLE TO SAVE TO THE UTTERMOST THOSE WHO COME TO GOD THROUGH HIM.
Hebrews 7:25

I believe; therefore, I speak.

...I LIVE BY FAITH IN THE SON OF GOD.
Galatians 2:20b

I live to the audience of One.

*"I TELL YOU THE TRUTH, ANYONE WHO BELIEVES IN ME
WILL DO THE SAME WORKS I HAVE DONE,
AND EVEN GREATER WORKS,
BECAUSE I AM GOING TO BE WITH THE FATHER."*
John 14:12 NLT

*IF YOU ARE WILLING AND OBEDIENT,
YOU WILL EAT THE GOOD OF THE LAND.*
Isaiah 1:9

If you can't accept anything by faith,
then you're doomed to a life dominated by doubt.

If you do not explore something in faith, you make room for unbelief.
Graham Cooke

If you don't fight giants, you will fight those that do.
If you don't fight demons, you will fight those that do.
Vlad Savchuk

If you feel 100% out of your realm of expertise, have hope!
Now it can be 100% His.

If you reach for a man's diagnosis, you will reach for a man's prognosis.
If you receive God's diagnosis, you will receive God's prognosis.
Zow

It is in a world where faith is difficult that faith exists.
Peter Kreeft, Boston College

Look at the enemy and declare. Look at Jesus and proclaim.
Graham Cooke

... MY RIGHTEOUS ONE SHALL LIVE BY FAITH;
AND IF HE SHRINKS BACK, MY SOUL HAS NO PLEASURE IN HIM.
Hebrews 10:38 NASB

Never move contrary to the inward witness of God's peace.
Pat Gastineau

Not faith or works; not faith and works; but faith that works.

NOW FAITH IS BEING SURE OF WHAT WE HOPE FOR...
Not then, not to be, but NOW.

Obedience is the place of God's provision for you.

Offense is the bond linked to deception.

One needs absolute faith. True faith confronts and is ignited by initiative.
Roberts Liardon, God's Generals

One of the greatest demonstrations of faith
is to grow amid grumblers, defectors, and murmurers.
Crane Brinton

Only a real risk tests the reality of a belief.
C. S. Lewis

Only what comes from above has the power to change what is beneath.

Personal obedience–not performance.

Rather than something you do, trust is a lack of resistance to a thing.
Zow

Read yourself full; think yourself straight; pray yourself hot; let yourself go.

Real faith built the ark, but real faith did not shut the door. God did that!
Smith Wigglesworth

Sacrifice releases power.

Show me what you do, and I will show you what you believe.

Suffering is not the worst thing that can happen to you, disobedience is.
Tom White, Voice of the Martyrs

The basic course of our lives is dictated by submission
to fear or submission to faith.

The professor does not talk while the student takes the test.

*THOSE WHO RECEIVE THE ABUNDANCE OF GRACE AND
OF THE GIFT OF RIGHTEOUSNESS WILL REIGN IN LIFE
THROUGH THE ONE, JESUS CHRIST.*
Romans 5:17

Those who remain under the law void faith.

True faith lives only as long as true love lives through us.

Walk in a vision that's so large that if God is not in it, it is destined to fail.
Presbyterian Church Sign

... *"WHAT IS IMPOSSIBLE WITH MAN IS POSSIBLE WITH GOD."*
Luke 28-27 BSB

What would you ask for if nothing or no one could disappoint you?
Zow

When the opportunity of a lifetime comes,
you must act within the lifetime of the opportunity.

When you go, you will know.

No doubt!

Nothing reveals the true character of a person like conflict.

6
TUG OF WAR
Before the Prize

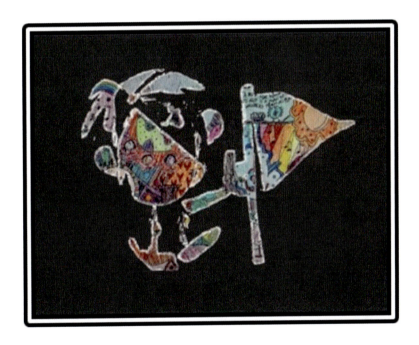

A person must decide beforehand that his integrity is not for sale.
Sally Reep

All is not as it seems.
Shared by Darrell Dahlman

All successful deliverance must begin by first removing that which defends the enemy.

ALL THE DAYS OF MY STRUGGLE
I WILL WAIT UNTIL MY CHANGE COMES.
Job 14:14 NASB

An overcomer's life is an essential life.

Appeasement is nothing more than surrender on the installment plan.
Dwight Eisenhower

Be careful not to take in everything that comes at you.
Test it to see if it's true.
Schatzie to Zow

Better is a live donkey than a dead lion.
Ernest Shackleton

Beware of small expenses. A small leak will sink a great ship.
Benjamin Franklin

Bitterness is about something you have lost. Envy wants something it does not have.

Bitterness is murder in diapers.

Constructive change offers the best method of avoiding destructive change.
Theodore Roosevelt

Courage does not always roar.
Mary A. Radmacher

Courage: Mental or moral strength to venture, persevere,
and withstand danger, fear, or difficulty.
Courage is meeting strain with fortitude and resilience.
It is having a firm determination to achieve one's end.

Defeat dwells in passivity.
Even when faith and hope are present, inaction will result in a battle lost.
Ana Mendez Ferrell, Regions of Captivity

Disapproval and the will to act were not linked in the American mind.
Nazi Refugees

Do not the greatest TESTimonies come out of the greatest tests?

Envy: Painful or resentful awareness of an advantage enjoyed by another
with a desire to possess the same advantage.

Every now and then the tree of liberty
must be watered with the blood of patriots and tyrants.
Thomas Jefferson, 1787

Everything is going to be alright if your everything is Jesus.

For the want of a nail, the war was lost.

God does not give us an overcoming life. He gives us life as we overcome.
Oswald Chambers

God never called us to criticize the darkness; He called us to cast it out.

*...HE STANDS AT THE RIGHT HAND OF THE NEEDY,
TO SAVE HIM FROM THOSE WHO JUDGE HIS SOUL.
Psalm 109:31 NASB*

*HUMBLE YOURSELVES THEREFORE UNDER THE MIGHTY HAND OF GOD,
THAT HE MAY EXALT YOU IN DUE SEASON.
1 Peter 5:6 KJV*

I know you can fight, but it's our wits that make us men.
Wallace's Father, Braveheart Movie

If a dead work comes against me, and I choose to carry the offense,
the defilement of that fleshly act would rot into me.
I have been set free to walk separated from dead works to
stand in the liberty of Christ.
Zow

IF THE RULER'S TEMPER RISES AGAINST YOU,
DO NOT ABANDON YOUR POSITION,
BECAUSE COMPOSURE ALLAYS GREAT OFFENSES.
Ecclesiastes 10:4 NASB

If God wanted to do it independently of us,
He would not have put the Holy Spirit within us.
Bobby Hamby

If men will not defend and fight for their own particular spot,
if they will not drive the enemy from their doors,
they deserve the slavery and subjection that awaits them.
Abigail Adams

If you become a people pleaser, the anointing of God withdraws from your life,
the tormentor sets in, and temptation's door is opened.
Vlad Savchuk

If you have gone one hundred miles from Jesus, it is not one hundred miles back.
Just turn around and He is right there.

In the end, we will remember not the words of our enemies, but the silence of our friends.
Martin Luther King, Jr.

In war, the main thing is to win the last battle, not the first.
Hirkani

In your headquarters, you are not to think defensively, only offensively.
Winston Churchill

Is prayer your steering wheel or your spare tire?
Corrie Ten Boom

Is there any soldier who would dare not face danger more boldly
under the eyes of his general? Only he who proves himself receives the prize.

It is not that truth is difficult to see that we make mistakes.
We make mistakes because the easiest and most comfortable course for
us is to seek insight where it accords with our emotions, primarily selfish ones.
Alex Solzhenitsyn, Russian novelist, 1918

Jealousy: Intolerant of rivalry or unfaithfulness;
hostile toward a rival or one believed to enjoy an advantage;
also vigilant guarding of a possession. God is a jealous God on my behalf.

LET NOT THE ONE WHO PUTS ON HIS ARMOR BOAST LIKE HIM WHO TAKES IT OFF.
I Kings 20:11b

Lust is content with nothing.

No opportunity presents itself twice the same.

Nothing in nature is perfectly in a straight line.

Nothing reveals the true character of a person like conflict.

Nothing ventured, nothing won!

*...OUT OF THE ABUNDANCE OF THE HEART
THE MOUTH SPEAKS.*
Matthew 12:34b

Pain is temporary. Quitting lasts forever.

Remember to play after every storm.
Mattie Stepanek

Some hit rock bottom before consulting God their Rock.
Stephen Boone

Storms give way to either peace or fear.

The enemy aims to capitalize on our emotions to
magnify his perspective onto our situations.
Zow

The enemy whispered, "You'll not be able to weather this storm!"
"Be still," I AM whispered back.

The mouth speaks out of that which fills the heart.

The purpose of war is occupation.
Napoleon Bonaparte

The will of God is often met with great adversity.

There are no rights without responsibility.

To be prepared for war is the most effective means to promote peace.
George Washington

True freedom often looks like bondage at first.
Bondage often looks like freedom at first.

Wars are fought over oil. Remember this!
It is the energy of the world's system and of the rich.
So also, in the Kingdom, the enemy of your spirit
strives to keep you from the Holy Spirit.
God to Zow

What you know got you here,
but it won't take you from here to where you want to go.
Alan Smith

Whatever I am provoked by in others is perhaps what God wants to deal with in me.
Zow

Whatever you compromise to keep you're going to lose.

When evil desires find you armed with the fear of God and determined to resist,
they will flee far away from you, and you will never see them again,
for they fear your weapons.

When for a moment a man is off guard,
in all probability, you will know more truth about him
than in all his attempts to reveal himself or hide himself.
Amplified Bible Note 1 Samuel 26

When truth meets your spirit but is not received,
at that point,
you have welcomed a spirit of error.

Whenever you have more than enough, you are rich.

Wisdom runs in the wells of the hearer. A hearer is a doer of the Word of God.

Worry is an unproductive use of a good imagination.

*YOU HAVE BECOME ESTRANGED FROM CHRIST,
YOU WHO ATTEMPT TO BE JUSTIFIED BY LAW;
YOU HAVE FALLEN FROM GRACE.*
Galatians 5:4

You must come to the end of yourself to find a beginning with God.

You're either in bondage or in the battle!
There is no middle ground.
Vlad Savchuk

TUG OF WAR - *Before the Prize*

Game on!

> *One day is all we have until we are given another.*
>
> *Zow*

7
TIGHTENING THE KNOTS
Common Sense

A poor worker always blames his tools.

An armed man is a citizen. An unarmed man is a subject.
John Adams

Anger is never without a reason, but seldom with a good one.
Benjamin Franklin

..."Childlike in simplicity and unselfish in character,
he remained unspoiled by praise and success...
the same in victory or defeat – calm and contained".
Reflections of General Lee by son, Captain Robert Lee

Did any kingdom or state ever regain their liberty, when once it was invaded,
without bloodshed? I cannot think of it without horror.
Abigail Adams, 1774

DOING WICKEDNESS IS LIKE SPORT TO A FOOL;
AND SO IS WISDOM TO A MAN OF UNDERSTANDING.
Proverbs 10:23 NASB

Excuses are the nails you use to build a house of failure.
Jim Rohn

False words are not only evil in themselves, but they infect the soul with evil.
Socrates

Focus on opportunities, not entitlements.

Having a ship on the sea is good but having the sea inside the ship–problem!

He that rises late must trot all day.
Benjamin Franklin

HE WHO ANSWERS A MATTER BEFORE HE HEARS IT, IT IS FOLLY AND SHAME TO HIM.
Proverbs 18:13

He who speaks cheaply proves he has never paid the price.
I like to see a man proud of the place in which he lives.
I like to see a man live in it so that the place will be proud of him.
Abraham Lincoln

I WILL SET NO WICKED THING BEFORE MY EYES;
I HATE THE WORK OF THOSE WHO FALL AWAY; IT SHALL NOT CLING TO ME.
Psalm 101:3

If guns kill people, then pencils misspell words,
cars make people drunk, and spoons make people fat.
Will Ferrell

IF THE AX IS DULL, AND ONE DOES NOT SHARPEN THE EDGE,
THEN HE MUST USE MORE STRENGTH; BUT WISDOM BRINGS SUCCESS.
Ecclesiastes 10:10

If you don't change, you become brittle.

If you don't want anyone to know, don't do it!
Chinese Proverb

Insignificant occurrences are sometimes advanced intimations of earth-shaking events. Sometimes we find that infinitude lies buried within the bosom of a trifle.
Evan Roberts, Welch Revivalist

IT IS GOOD THAT YOU GRASP ONE THING WHILE NOT LETTING GO OF THE OTHER; FOR ONE WHO FEARS GOD COMES OUT WITH BOTH OF THEM.
Ecclesiastes 7:18 NASB

Laugh every day – it's like inner jogging.
Norman Cousins

Leave a place better than you found it.

Let your word be your bond.

Life's tough – get a helmet.
Candace Owens

Like fish that live in water, poverty lives in ignorance.

Live below your means.

Love never fails; not loving always fails.

Love only exists where there is freedom.

Keep your face to the sunshine and you cannot see a shadow.
Helen Keller

Maturity is working through your trauma and not
using it as a never-ending excuse for your poor behavior.
Ellis Anthony

Men do not fear bondage; they fear freedom
for in absolute freedom comes the responsibility to choose.

Money is not the answer, but neither is it the problem.

Never miss a good opportunity to shut up.
Will Rogers

Never surrender the sense of His presence to your situation.

No man steps in the same river twice.
Heraclitus

No pain, no gain.
Benjamin Franklin

Nothing happens until something moves.
Albert Einstein

Other people don't determine your attitude, they only reveal it.
Shared by Dan King

Others may; you cannot.
Schatzie

Our hearts of stone become hearts of flesh when we learn where the outcast weeps,
Brennan Manning

Pain is temporary, quitting lasts forever.
Lance Armstrong

Pay your bills on time.

Poor planning on your part does not necessitate an emergency on mine.
Bob Carter

POVERTY AND SHAME WILL COME TO HIM WHO DISDAINS CORRECTION,
BUT HE WHO REGARDS A REBUKE WILL BE HONORED.
Proverbs 13:18

PRIDE GOES BEFORE DESTRUCTION, A HAUGHTY SPIRIT BEFORE A FALL.
Proverbs 16:18 NIV

Seize the day.

Show respect to all people and grovel to none.
Chief Tecumseh

Some people say, some people do.

Sometimes less is more.

The grass may be greener on the other side, but so is the water bill.

THE HEART OF HIM WHO HAS UNDERSTANDING SEEKS KNOWLEDGE, BUT THE MOUTH OF FOOLS FEEDS ON FOOLISHNESS
Proverbs 15:14

The only true wisdom is knowing you know nothing.
Socrates

There's nothing wrong with having stuff,
but when the stuff has you, everything is wrong.
Zow

Those who would give up essential liberty to purchase a little temporary safety
deserves neither liberty nor safety.
Benjamin Franklin

We cannot be happy without being free.
We cannot be free without being secure in our property.
We know too well the blessings of freedom to tamely resign it.
John Dickinson, 1732-1808

We need to build our immunity to taking offense
so that we can deal with the issues that justified criticism can raise.
Rowan Atkinson

We think and improve our judgments by committing our thoughts to paper.
John Adams to Quincy Adams

Well done is better than well said.
Benjamin Franklin

What do you want to be known for? What makes a person great?
What do you believe is the most lasting element of life?

What I spent, I had. What I saved, I lost. What I gave, I have.
Old German Motto

What is hateful to you, do not do to your neighbor.
Hillel

Whatever you do, do not take the precious things, and make them common.
Zow|

When the opportunity of a lifetime comes,
you must act within the lifetime of the opportunity.
Leonard Ravenhill

When you do the right thing,
you take care of people.
When you take care of people,
you compromise on the right thing.
Shared by Sally Reep

When you have something to say, silence is a lie.
Jordan Peterson

When you know better, do better.

WHO IS THE MAN WHO FEARS THE LORD?
HIM WILL HE INSTRUCT IN THE WAY THAT HE SHOULD CHOOSE
Proverbs 25:12 ESV

WHOEVER DIGS A PIT WILL FALL INTO IT,
AND HE WHO ROLLS A STONE, IT WILL COME BACK ON HIM.
Proverbs 26:27

Without free speech, there is no true thought.
Jordan Peterson

You can avoid reality, but you cannot avoid the consequences of reality.
Ayn Rand

You deserve whatever you tolerate.
Henry Cloud

You don't train for a race at the finish line.

You should not honor men more than truth.
Plato

Your future is not connected to those that left, but those who stayed.
Vlad Savchuk

Your mission is sure! Do not find solace in poor companions.
God to Zow

No Brainer!

Have I judged yesterday an imprisoned tomorrow?

Zow

8
ROPE BURN
Told You So's

A lie is a lie. Deception swallowed is unbelief.
God to Zow

Am I building a coping mechanism for something God wants to destroy?

Anger is the vacuum of desire.

Any overemphasis of any one particular spiritual truth becomes spiritual error.
Kathryn Kuhlman

Backsliding is not going backwards as much as it is
me standing still when God is going forward.

BAD COMPANY CORRUPTS GOOD MORALS.
1 Corinthians 15:33 NASB

Be yourself. Everyone else is already taken.
Oscar Wilde

Because of the passion of Christ, loneliness is now a choice.

BEHOLD, HAPPY IS THE MAN WHOM GOD CORRECTS.
THEREFORE, DO NOT DESPISE THE CHASTENING OF THE ALMIGHTY.
Job 5:17

Bondage is any person, place, or thing, by relationship,
that prevents you from fulfilling your purpose in Christ Jesus.

Could it be that every temptation, disappointment, sin, or bondage
is rooted in the singular lie that God is not good?
Shared by Sandi Robinson

Dead works know no lasting joy!
Zow

Depression is the deception that comes from seeing the world
from your own perspective.
Zow

Divisive thinking operates from the tree of knowledge of good and evil.
Zow

Do not ever entrust more than what you can afford to lose.
Mary Jean Duggan

Don't piss in my ear and call it rain.
Mary Jean Duggan

Don't sell the sun to buy a candle.
Jewish Proverb

Expectations are premeditated disappointments.

False comforts produce shame. God's comfort produces grace.
Beth Moore

*FOR BY WHOM A MAN IS OVERCOME,
BY HIM ALSO HE IS BROUGHT INTO BONDAGE.
2 Peter 2:19b*

God can give a straight blow with a crooked stick.
Corrie Ten Boom

Good intentions do not equal obedience.

Have I judged yesterday and imprisoned tomorrow?
Zow

*HOW CAN YOU BELIEVE, WHO RECEIVE GLORY ONE FROM ANOTHER:
AND THE GLORY WHICH IS FROM GOD ALONE,
YOU DO NOT SEEK?.
John 5:44 Douay-Rheims Bible*

Hypocrisy is not acting against your feelings, but it is acting against your beliefs.

Idolatry rips boundaries to shreds.

IT IS GOOD FOR ME TO BE AFFLICTED, SO THAT I MAY LEARN YOUR STATUTES.
Psalm 119:71

Legalism is holiness without love.

Many are seeking to better their lives with God's help
without losing their lives for God's sake.

Marxism is slavery: You give everything to us, and we will take care of you.

May it never be said of me,
"I never met someone who knew so much but carried his knowledge so lightly."

My dead works are things I do to either alleviate my conscience or to get even with it.

Once again, defense of the rights of a weak state,
outraged and invaded by unprovoked aggression, forced us to draw the sword.
Once again, we must fight for life and honor,
against all might and fury of the valiant, disciplined, and ruthless (German) race,
once again, so be it.
Winston Churchill

*ONE HANDFUL OF REST IS BETTER THAN TWO FIST FULLS
OF LABOR AND STRIVING AFTER THE WIND.*
Ecclesiastes 4:6 NASB

Our measure of an infraction of a sinner to another sinner
is insignificant in comparison to a sinner to the Perfect One.

Pharisees are dream thieves.

REPROOFS FOR DISCIPLINE ARE THE WAY OF LIFE.
Proverbs 6:23b NASB

Satan does not read our minds; he reads our attitudes.

Secondhand revelation accompanied by secondhand faith
quickly evaporates, is untested, and is often unusable.
Zow

Sickness is the vengeance of nature for the violation of her laws.
Larry Randolph

Sin will take you farther than you ever thought you would go,
keep you longer than you ever thought you'd stay,
and cost you more than you ever thought you'd pay.
Ravi Zaccharias

Suffering hollows out space for God to fill.

The Church is called to be the world's thermostat, not its thermometer.

The difference between a sheep and a pig?
A pig falls in the mud and wants to stay there.
A sheep cries to get out and be cleaned up.

The enemy of our soul offers substitutes for spiritual hunger
with two extreme conditions–extreme heights of pride and
provision or extreme accusation. I offer My children My presence.
God to Zow

The great masses of people will fall more readily for a big lie than a small one.
Adolph Hitler

The Kingdom of God is about multiplication,
the flesh is about subtraction, and the devil is about division.
Zow

The lies of the enemy make my problems appear bigger than the solutions they carry.

The mountains you are carrying, you were only meant to climb.
Najwa Zebian

The proud are gods unto themselves.

The vanity of humanity believes we are here by some intrinsic power apart from God.

There are ditches on either side of the narrow path.
If you fall into one, don't try to figure out how to get out.
Your own way got you there.
Call on the Good Shepherd Who can save your soul.
Rick Joyner

There are no great men.
There are only great challenges which ordinary people are forced by circumstances to meet.
Admiral Wm. Frederick Halsey, Jr., U.S. Navy

Those who are under the law void faith.
Joseph Prince

To misunderstand or underrate the nature of evil is to resign or be blindsided by it.

Unsanctified mercy is rooted in bitterness.

Unsanctified mercy results in the justification of things the Lord desires to condemn or extract.
Paul Keith Davis

We experience loneliness when:
We try to fix the past or control the future,
We want to get things perfect,
We focus on shame from within.

What one generation tolerates; the next generation will embrace.
John Wesley

What you cannot enforce do not demand.
Sophocles

What you honestly confess to God is vanquishable.

When you're offended, you're setting yourself up for deception.
John Hammer

Whoever ponders is sure to wander in the paths the wonder goes.
Zow

Whomever we defend ourselves against, we allow to become our judge.

*WHY DO YOU ALSO TRANSGRESS THE COMMANDMENT
OF GOD BECAUSE OF YOUR TRADITION?*
Matthew 15:3

Wounds: Open places that don't yet hold the grace of God.
May God heal the festering parts of me...
May Your grace turn my wounds into scars and
my scars into testimonies.
Zow

*YET GOD DOES NOT TAKE AWAY LIFE;
BUT HE DEVISES WAYS THAT THE BANISHED ONE
MAY NOT BE CAST OUT FROM HIM.*
2 Samuel 14:14 BSB

You aren't learning anything when you're talking.
Lyndon B. Johnson

You can only receive what you think you're worth.

You cannot confess a wound as a sin.
Floyd McClung

You do not throw the whole thing away just because it's banged up a bit.
Seabiscuit Movie

You must hate evil to overcome evil.

Dang!

To be loved is the greatest need.

To know love is the greatest fulfillment.

To give love is the greatest commandment.

Zow

9
A BRAIDED LIFE
True Disciple

A Bible falling apart belongs to someone who is not.
Joseph Prince

A strong light offends weak eyes.

A wayward generation believes in "choice".
Even God didn't parent this way.
Choice was simply the opportunity to prove man's loyalty to Him.
Zow

All that comforts the flesh weakens the spirit.
Frances J. Roberts, Come Away, My Beloved

...ALL WHO DESIRE TO LIVE GODLY IN CHRIST JESUS WILL SUFFER PERSECUTION.
2 Timothy 3:12

AM I NOW SEEKING THE APPROVAL OF MEN, OR OF GOD?
OR AM I STRIVING TO PLEASE MEN?
IF I WERE STILL STRIVING TO PLEASE MEN,
I WOULD NOT BE A BONDSERVANT OF CHRIST.
Galatians 6:10 BSB

An un-preached gospel is no gospel at all.

Anything that happens too fast or too easily is often insignificant.

As you are in death, so must you be in life.
God to Zow

Be certain before wiping the dust off your feet that the offense
is on the rejection of truth and not the rejected.
Zow

Be difficult to offend and quick to forgive.

Behold how great a matter a little fire kindles.
Evan John Roberts, Welch Revivalist, 1904

Conversion, as God sees it, means that Christ and the Holy Spirit dwells in every believer
and overcomes in him all evil, ill temper, malice, arrogance, and lust.
Early Christians

Do you know you are a word from heaven?

Does one dare offend the intolerance of "tolerance"? If my Lord did, so shall I.
Zow

Expectation for life in anyone or anything other than God is idolatry.

Give it! Expect nothing in return.

Glory: Giving a good opinion about God.

God already has your stupidness factored into His plan.
Steve Bressler

...GOD'S FIRM FOUNDATION STANDS, BEARING THIS SEAL:
"THE LORD KNOWS THOSE WHO ARE HIS," AND,
"LET EVERYONE WHO NAMES THE NAME OF THE LORD DEPART FROM INIQUITY."
2 Timothy 2:19 ESV

Grace is counter-human.
It deceives my pride and reveals me.
Grace is revealed in Jesus Christ.
It explains true God and redeems me.
Zow

He lived not unto man, but unto God!
He lived not for man, but for God!
Zow

HE WHO KEEPS A ROYAL COMMAND EXPERIENCES NO TROUBLE,
FOR A WISE HEART KNOWS THE PROPER TIME AND PROCEDURE.
Ecclesiastes 8:5 NASB

He who truly possesses the Word of Jesus Christ can even hear His silence speak.
He will act in accordance with His words and will also be known by His silence.
Ignatius, Early Christian

Humility is agreement with God.

Humility is occupation with Christ, not self.
Humility isn't thinking less of yourself,
it's thinking about yourself less.
C.S. Lewis

I am predestined to be conformed into the likeness of God's Son.

I hold back nothing from You. All I need is in You. Even so Lord, come!
Zow

I would rather be a fool for Christ than a tool for the devil.

If it isn't in His mouth, it shouldn't be in mine.

If you are committed to the fire, you cannot negotiate the flames.

If you knew what I know about Jesus, I would want you to tell me.
Jesus Freaks

If your "asker" is broken, so is your "doer."
Zow

...It is either going forward or backward.
We refuse to go backward! We refuse to let the devil
throw the dust of time in our eyes and blind us to eternity.
Leonard Ravenhill

LET THOSE WHO LOVE HIM BE LIKE THE SUN
WHEN IT COMES OUT IN FULL STRENGTH.
Judges 5:31b

NOW ACQUAINT YOURSELF WITH HIM AND BE AT PEACE;
THEREBY GOOD WILL COME TO YOU.
Job 22:21

Obedience without delay is the quickest path to understanding.

Obey what I hear! Hear what I obey!
Zow

Patient waiting is often the highest form of doing God's will.

Possessions block our vision.
Mother Teresa

Pray in the Spirit at all times. Keep yourself in the love of God.

Preach the gospel always.

Prophetic people have a lifestyle of agreeing with God.

Rarely does one observe a singular star in the sky.
They are observed in relation one to another in the backdrop of darkness.
Even so, men of darkness will know we are disciples by our love for one another.

Sacrifice: Putting off immediate fulfillment when I understand
that there are eternal implications.

Say little. Do much.

Security is not found in the absence of danger, but in the presence of Jesus.

Show me what you do, and I'll show you what you believe.

Supernatural food didn't cause the children of Israel to live supernaturally.

The Spirit of God moves upon men, not movements.
When men respond to God, they are used to launch movements that involve
others in winning multitudes into the Kingdom of Heaven.
Steve Dursoff, Pentecost Behind Iron Curtain

The world was my oyster.
Shakespeare

The ultimate measure of a man is not where he stands in moments of comfort
and convenience, but where he stands in times of challenge.

The water carved the stone only because it fell...
drop by drop,
year after year,
without pause.
Had the accumulated water poured down at once in a powerful stream,
it would have slipped off the rock without leaving a trace.
Meditate Daily!

There are no simple answers, but there is love,
and love transforms what the mind cannot form.
God to Zow

Think before you speak. Read before you think.
Fran Lebowitz

This period we are now in is only a dressing room for all eternity.
Leonard Ravenhill

To be a Christian without prayer is no more possible than to be alive without air.
Martin Luther

To be a receiver is to be one who accepts Who God is: a giver.
Zow

To be loved is the greatest need.
To know love is the greatest fulfillment.
To give love is the greatest commandment.
Zow

To sing is to pray twice.

Until I know who I am in God, what good would it do to be or do something for God?
We are at our strongest point when we respond to God, not react to evil.
Bill Johnson

We are freed from something to Someone.

What are you willing to live for? What are you willing to die for?
What will you do with the life Jesus paid for?

*WHAT DOES THE LORD REQUIRE OF YOU BUT TO DO JUSTLY,
TO LOVE MERCY,
AND TO WALK HUMBLY WITH YOUR GOD?*
Micah 6:8

What is the fruit of an apple tree? Is it not another apple tree?

What Jesus suffered to give; do I eagerly receive?

Whatever God calls me to He first reveals Himself as able to meet my needs.
I must receive the Word of Who He is to position my heart to
receive the promises that He gives.
Zow

When God blesses you, it's usually with an opportunity.
Alan Smith

When God calls from the deep, don't answer from the shallow.

When Jesus calls a man, he bids him come and die.
Dietrich Bonhoeffer

When you hate your sin as He hates it, victory is sure.

Who do You want to be for me now that You couldn't be for me at any other time?
Graham Cooke

You are my Moment if you truly are my Life.
Zow

YOU ASK AND DO NOT RECEIVE,
BECAUSE YOU ASK AMISS,
THAT YOU MAY SPEND IT ON YOUR OWN PLEASURES.
James 4:3

You can kill us, but you cannot do us any real harm.
Justin Martyr, 165 A.D.

You do not believe grace until you minister it.

You do not have the chance to submit to authority until
you disagree with that authority.

You intended it for harm, but God intended it for good,
to accomplish what is now being done,
the saving of many souls.
Joseph, 1689 B.C.

You know for a while you carry the cross, but after a while, the cross carries you.

You must serve a Laban before you serve an Abraham.
Graham Cooke

You never know how much you really believe anything until it's
truth or falsehood becomes a matter of life and death to you.
C.S. Lewis

You should utter words as though heaven were opened within them,
and as though you did not put the word into your mouth,
but as though you had entered the Word.
Martin Buber, Jewish Philosopher

You thought you were going to be a decent little cottage, but He is building a palace.
C.S. Lewis

Your actions speak so loudly I cannot hear what you are saying.
Ralph Waldo Emerson

Your test of humility is your attitude toward subordinates.

ALL IN!

> *I play songs, but really, they play me.*
>
> Zow

10
LEARN THE ROPES
Talents

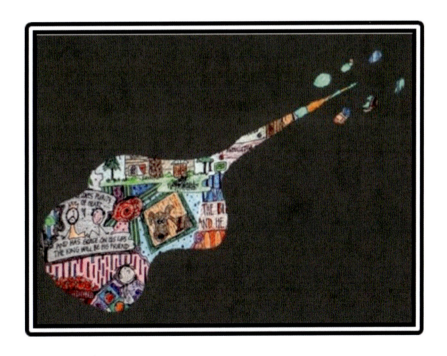

LEARN THE ROPES - *Talents*

A hundred times every day I remind myself that
my inner and outer life depend on the labors of other men, living and dead,
and I must exert myself to give the same measure
I have received and am still receiving.
Albert Einstein

A talent is formed in stillness. A character in the world's torrent.
Goethe

An artist draws what he sees, not what he knows.

Anything that happens too fast or too easily is usually insignificant.

Art is the revenge of the human spirit over and against the small-minded.
Nat King Cole's daughter, Natalie

Brevity is the art of genius.
Zow

Coram Deo laboramus: We work in the sight of God.

Crossroads: Where passion meets purpose.

DO YOU SEE A MAN WHO EXCELS IN HIS WORK?
HE WILL STAND BEFORE KINGS;
HE WILL NOT STAND BEFORE UNKNOWN MEN.
Proverbs 22:29

Don't only practice your art but force your way into its secrets;
art deserves that, for it and knowledge can raise man to the divine.
Ludwig van Beethoven

Don't sell the sun to buy a candle.
Jewish Proverb

EACH OF YOU SHOULD USE WHATEVER GIFT YOU HAVE RECEIVED
TO SERVE OTHERS, AS FAITHFUL STEWARDS OF
GOD'S GRACE IN ITS VARIOUS FORMS.
I Peter 4:10 NIV

Every noble work is at first impossible.
Thomas Carlyle

Every obstacle has an opportunity.

Excuses are the nails you use to build your house of failure.
Jim Rohn

HARDWORKING FARMERS HAVE MORE THAN ENOUGH FOOD;
DAYDREAMERS ARE NOTHING MORE THAN STUPID FOOLS.
Proverbs 12:11 CEV

He who works with his hands, his head, and his heart is an artist.
St. Francis of Assisi

Hide not your talents, they for use were made; what's a sundial in the shade?
Benjamin Franklin

I play songs, but really, they play me.
Zow

If you want something you have never had,
you must be willing to do something you have never done.
Thomas Jefferson

It takes courage to grow up and become who you really are.
B.E. Cummings

Necessity is indeed the mother of invention.
Albert Einstein

No man is greater than his prayer life.
Leonard Ravenhill

No tears in the writer, no tears in the reader.
Robert Frost

One does not write what has already been written.

One who is shy will not learn.
Hillel, Jewish Teacher

Passion will always take you further than talent ever will.

Purpose: The reason for which something exists or is done or made useful.

Risk only as much as you can lose.
Remember, the single talent man risked nothing and lost everything.

The artist is nothing without the gift, but the gift is nothing without the work.
Emile Zola

The greatest tragedy in life is men living with sight but no vision.
Helen Keller

THE SOUL OF THE SLUGGARD CRAVES AND GETS NOTHING,
WHILE THE SOUL OF THE DILIGENT IS RICHLY SUPPLIED.
Proverbs 13:4 ESV

Those who dream by day are cognizant of many things which
escape those who dream only by night.
Edgar Allen Poe

To live a creative life, we must lose our fear of being wrong.
Joseph Chilton Pearce

To play a wrong note is insignificant. To play without passion is inexcusable.
Ludwig van Beethoven

Understanding and goodness matter more than intellect.

Well-directed imaginations are the source of great deeds.

What is in my hands to do?

When the student is ready, the teacher appears.
Lao Tzu

WHOEVER IS FAITHFUL WITH VERY LITTLE
WILL ALSO BE FAITHFUL WITH MUCH.
AND WHOEVER IS DISHONEST WITH VERY LITTLE
WILL ALSO BE DISHONEST WITH MUCH.
Luke 16:10 BSB

Work hard in silence; let your success be your noise.
Frank Ocean

You can judge the power of an idea by the resistance it creates.
You know what you value by what you make time for.
C.J. Mahaney

*YOU MUST REMEMBER THE LORD YOUR GOD,
FOR HE IS THE ONE WHO GIVES ABILITY TO GET WEALTH.*
Deuteronomy 8:18 NET

You positively need to be occupied with something weighty,
deep, profound, and difficult.
Jordan Peterson

You shall cease writing if you cease learning.
You do not learn as you write but write as you learn.
God to Zow

You will never plow the field if you only turn it over in your mind.
Irish Proverb

You've got to get up every morning with determination
if you're going to go to bed with satisfaction.
George Lorimer

LEARN THE ROPES - *Talents*

Your dreams miss you!

Your talent is God's gift to you; what you do with it is your gift to God.
Leo Buscaglia

Your talents are a down payment on your destiny.
Matshona Dhliwayo

Youth is the time to improve the mind.
Be diligent to improve yourself in every line of useful knowledge;
so that in future years, you may be a blessing to all those
with whom you may come in contact and
all those to whom it may be your privilege to serve.
W.T. McRee, 1947

LEARN THE ROPES - *Talents*

Rookies Rock!

> *Brilliance defined by man is intelligence.*
>
> *Brilliance defined by God is surrender.*
>
> *Zow*

11
STRONG STRANDS

Strong Stands

A life of luxury weakens the spirit; frugality makes it strong.
Municius Felix

AND THE WORK OF RIGHTEOUSNESS WILL BE PEACE,
AND THE EFFECT OF RIGHTEOUSNESS, QUIETNESS AND ASSURANCE FOREVER.
Isaiah 32:17

Be aware of what exalts you.

Be not afraid of growing slowly, be afraid of standing still.
Chinese Proverb

Be the same as you do; never do what Jesus says to never do.

BLESSED ARE THE PURE IN HEART, FOR THEY SHALL SEE GOD.
Matthew 5:8

Brilliance defined by man is intelligence.
Brilliance defined by God is surrender.
Zow

Criticalness is evidence of pride.

Departures come by distraction via volition or violation.
Distractions are most easily curbed by intent.
Zow

Do I have an unholy alliance with comfort?

Do not condemn yourself!
Celebrate another chance to humbly fall into your Savior's most excellent grace.
His hand will bear you up from shame to face Him once again.

Do not fail to enter the door. I open or be held back by feelings of unreadiness.
I am your preparation.
God to Zow

Don't let the fears regarding tomorrow drain my today.

Don't say things. What you are stands over you the while,
and thunders so that I cannot hear what you say to the contrary.
Ralph Waldo Emerson

Drink in silence. Seek solitude. Listen to the silence. It will teach you.
It will build strength. Let others share it with you. It is priceless.
God to Zow

Fellowship with God was Adam's purpose in life.
Dale Fife

God has not called us to be successful. He has called us to be faithful.
Mother Teresa

God instituted and defined the covenant of marriage.
He has not changed the script.
Zow

*GREAT PEACE HAVE THEY THAT LOVE THY LAW,
AND NOTHING SHALL OFFEND THEM*
Psalm 119:165

Happiness is being, not having.

Hasten to perform the trivial duty that it may bring you to a great one.
Jewish Proverb

*HE WHO IS SLOW TO ANGER IS BETTER THAN THE MIGHTY;
AND HE WHO RULES OVER HIS SPIRIT
THAN HE WHO CAPTURES A CITY.*
Proverbs 16:32

I am ruthless in My quest to eradicate all that obstructs love,
for truth cannot penetrate what love does not facilitate.
God to Zow

If water, which is soft, can hollow out a stone which is hard,
how much more the Words of Torah, which are hard, cut through and
make an impression on my heart, which is soft.
Rabbi Akiva ben Joseph

If you're not at peace with God, you won't be at peace with His miracles.
Rolland Baker

In matters of style, swim with the current. In matters of principle, stand like a rock.
Thomas Jefferson

...IN THE SCROLL OF THE BOOK, IT IS WRITTEN OF ME,
I DELIGHT TO DO THY WILL, OH MY GOD.
AND YOUR LAW IS WITHIN MY HEART.
Psalm 40:7-8

Is my internal reality greater than my external circumstances?
The storms that give way will either produce fear or peace.

It is a sad fate for a man to be too well known to everyone else
but unknown to himself.
Francis Bacon

Joy is non-negotiable.

Knowledge isn't power until it's applied.

No one is without difficulties,
and everyone knows best where their own shoe pinches.
Abigail Adams

Olympians aren't made in a day,
but Olympians give themselves daily to being made.
Zow

Preparation is to say "yes" to whatever God ordains for us.

Sacrifice something temporary for something eternal.

Security is not found in the absence of danger, but in the presence of Jesus.
Take no thought for your life, for the heavenly Father cares for you!

*SOW FOR YOURSELF RIGHTEOUSNESS;
REAP IN MERCY; BREAK UP YOUR FALLOW GROUND;
FOR IT IS TIME TO SEEK THE LORD TILL HE COMES TO RAIN RIGHTEOUSNESS ON YOU.*
Hosea 10:12

Speak softly and carry a big stick.
Teddy Roosevelt

Studying increases one's capacity for joy.

The best love from God you can receive is when you feel the most vulnerable.

The best part of valor is discretion.
Shakespeare

The best way to break down barriers between people and communities are through simple, unforced acts of kindness. One act can undo years of estrangement.
Rabbi Jonathan Sacks

The born-again heart is a virgin that has many suitors.

The inward man responds to God. The outward man reacts to circumstances.
Graham Cooke

The secret of happiness is freedom. And the secret of freedom is courage.
Gilbert Murray

There is no breakthrough without follow-through.

Though modesty is a virtue, bashfulness is a vice.
Benjamin Franklin

Voluntary simplicity involves both inner and other conditions...a singleness of purpose, sincerity, and honesty within, as well as the avoidance of exterior clutter, of many possessions irrelevant to the chief purpose of life. It means an ordering and guiding of our energy and our desires; a partial restraint in some directions to secure greater abundance of life in other directions.
It involves a deliberate organization of life for a purpose.
Richard Gregg, 1936

We are born into this world looking for Someone looking for us
and we never stop searching until we find Him.

Whatever in my history that I am holding away from myself,
or not owning, and not rewriting into victory, continues to recycle in my current relationships.
Anne Nesbit

Whatever overshadows you will be released in your shadow.
Bill Johnson

When I judge what God is not judging, I put deception and deafness over my own ears.
Anne Nesbit

When we learn to be trustworthy, the Lord often heaps blessings.
Stripping of blessings is often to test our trust.
Charles Stanley

Unto You, my Lord!

> *As He is inexhaustible, so is His love!*
>
> *Zow*

12
THE TIES THAT BIND

Love Wins

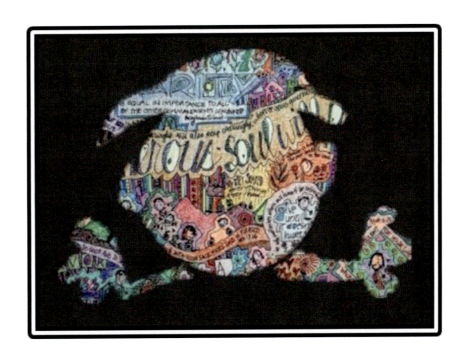

THE TIE THAT BIND - *Love Wins*

As I am in this world, so shall you be! Love them!
God to Zow

Be kind, for everyone you meet is fighting a harder battle.
Plato

Do you see? Do you see?
All the people sinking down?
Don't you care? Don't you care?
Are you gonna let them drown?
Keith Green, Musician

Err on the side of life and love.
Zow

Everything I understand, I understand only because I love.
Leo Tolstoy

Gather instead and practice in seeking out what serves the common good.
Woe to those who are wise in their own estimation
and clever in their own conceit.
Unknown Early Church Father

Give it all and expect nothing in return.

If people fear to offer criticism lest it lead to a rupture of peace,
that in itself proves the peace is false.
Peace, if it is to last, must be based on truth and lack of fear.
Rabbi Joseph Telushkin, Jewish Wisdom

If we pray, we believe. If we believe, we will. If we love, we will serve.
Mother Teresa

If you can't say anything nice, don't say anything at all.
Quote used by Elizabeth McRee

If you would love, be lovable.

Is it true; is it necessary; is it kind?
Quote used by Schatzie

Jesus would rather suffer God's wrath for me than live in heaven without me.

Legalism is holiness without love.

*LET US CONSIDER HOW TO STIR UP ONE ANOTHER
TO LOVE AND GOOD WORKS.*
Hebrew 10:24

Life in the Spirit is spontaneous because love is spontaneous.
Oswald Chambers

Life is mostly froth and bubbles. Only two things stand like stone.
Kindness in another man's troubles. Courage in your own.
Adam Lindsay Gordon

Love is our greatest weapon. Humility is our greatest protection.
Zow

Love is the source of courage.
Rick Joyner

Love me wild!
I promise my heart will bloom for you.
Alexandra Vasiliu

Love unaccompanied by criticism is not love.
Peace unaccompanied by reproof is not peace.
Genesis Rabbah 54.3

Measure your life in seasons of love.

Men who are truth-filled with light are those who
have deeply gazed into the darkness of their imperfect existence.
Brennan Manning

No sin is found in true selfless love.

Only people capable of loving strongly can suffer great sorrow,
but this same necessity of loving serves to counteract their grief and heals them.
Leo Tolstoy

PERFECT LOVE CASTS OUT FEAR.
John 4:18

Reach out to the unlovely.
Schatzie

Root out all that is in me that obstructs love.
Zow

The way of mercy takes me to the least.
David Ruis, Musician

There is a difference between love and approval.
John Ruttkay

There is the land of the living and the land of the dead.
The bridge is the cross of Jesus.

To know the needs of men and to bear their burden of sorrow,
that is the true love of men.
Martin Buber

Trust is the fruit of a relationship in which we perceive we are loved.

Vulnerability: Weakness with trust.

We are not changed by knowledge but by love.
Only the heart that is melted in devotion is pliable in My hand.
Only the mind that is open to the Spirit can receive divine revelation.
God to Zow

We cannot love from self as a source because human love requires a reason.
God loves without reason! His love is the only love that can love an enemy.
Zow

We make a living by what we get. We make a life by what we give.
Ronald W. Reagan

We measure the quality of our lives by the depth of our relationships.
Rolland Baker

What I needed most was to love and to be loved, eager to be caught.
Happily, I wrapped those painful bonds around me; and sure enough,
I would be lashed with the red-hot pokers of jealousy,
by suspicions and fear, by bursts of anger and quarrels.
Saint Augustine

What the eye doesn't see, the heart doesn't grieve over.
Paulo Coelho

What we don't say in words, we ultimately say in deeds.
Beth Moore

When the soul gives up all for love so that it can have Him,
that is all, then it finds true rest.
Julian of Norwich

Years of the Holy Spirit's friendship culminate into eternity.
As He is inexhaustible, so is His love!
Zow

You alone, my Lord, can redeem all my hiding places from
the lie that love is unable to reach my devastations.
Zow

You will not find boredom in love;
there is no exercise that completely exhausts its wonder.
Zow

Your love, Oh God, is my blessed life.
Zow

Seventy times seven!

Presented opportunities give way to prove with actions the quality and genuineness of your words.

Zow

13

TIED THE KNOT

Marriage

A happy marriage is the union of two good forgivers.
Ruth Graham

A HOUSE DIVIDED AGAINST ITSELF WILL NOT STAND.
Matthew 12:25b

A man doesn't own his marriage, he is only steward of his wife's love.
Ed Cole

A marriage marked by heaven is targeted by hell.

A rut is nothing but an open grave with both ends kicked out.
Earl Nightingale

AN EXCELLENT WIFE IS THE CROWN OF HER HUSBAND,
BUT SHE WHO BRINGS HIM SHAME IS LIKE ROTTENNESS TO HIS BONES.
Proverbs 12:4 ESV

Anger is a motivating emotion that should promote us to action, not a cycle of anger.

Are you willing to remain right where you are and let the Lord do great things through you, though no man may seem to notice at all?
Keith Green

AS FOR ME AND MY HOUSE, WE WILL SERVE THE LORD.
Joshua 24:15

"BE ANGRY, YET DO NOT SIN":
DO NOT LET THE SUN GO DOWN ON YOUR WRATH,
NOR GIVE PLACE TO THE DEVIL.
Ephesians 4:26-27

BUT I SAY TO YOU THAT WHOEVER DIVORCES HIS WIFE FOR ANY REASON
EXCEPT SEXUAL IMMORALITY CAUSES HER TO COMMIT ADULTERY;
AND WHOEVER MARRIES A WOMAN WHO IS DIVORCED COMMITS ADULTERY.
Matthew 5:32

CATCH THE FOXES FOR US, THE LITTLE FOXES THAT SPOIL THE VINEYARDS,
FOR OUR VINEYARDS ARE IN BLOSSOM.
Song of Solomon 2:15 ESV

For a wife, take the daughter of a good mother.
Thomas Fuller

Good sex is the result of a tree well-tended, not a tree well-selected.

GREAT PEACE HAVE THEY THAT LOVE THY LAW:
AND NOTHING SHALL OFFEND THEM.
Psalm 119:165 KJV

Happiness is being, not having.

Having a child is like having your heart walking about outside your body.
Zow

Home is the touchstone you return to when life is filled with changes
and you need some time to redefine your role.
Mary Engelbreit

How much you disclose and how much you are accepted
in that disclosure equals intimacy.

I am not going to follow signs, but rather the peace of God. Signs will follow me.
Jessica Wilmot

I positively forbid any connection between my daughter and any youth
upon earth who does not totally eradicate every taste for gaiety and expense.
John Adams to Wife, Abigail regarding daughter, Nabby

If you are wrong, speak up! If you are right, shut up.
Pastor Tom Nesbitt, Iowa

If you really want the last word in a petty argument, try saying,
"I guess you're right."

Intentional godly parenting is one of the most courageous
enlistments a soul can undertake.
Zow

It is by the female world that the greatest and best character among men is formed.
When I hear of an extraordinary man, I naturally inquire, who is the mother?
There can be nothing in life more honorable for a woman than to contribute
by her virtue and advice and her example to the formation of a
husband, a brother, or a son to be useful to the world.
Abigail Adams

Joy that isn't shared, I've heard, dies young.

*LET MARRIAGE BE HELD IN HONOR AMONG ALL
AND LET THE MARRIAGE BED BE UNDEFILED,
FOR GOD WILL JUDGE THE SEXUALLY IMMORAL AND ADULTEROUS.*
Hebrews 13:4 ESV

Love is unconditional. Trust is earned.

Lovers do not want expectations, they want presence.

Marital relationships are not for our partner's pleasure only,
but for the birthing of natural and spiritual seed
on the earth for God's good pleasure.

Marriage: One of God's powerful secret weapons for revolutionizing the human heart.

Marital stakes: While the sense of independence is diminished,
that of individuality is fulfilled.
Zondervan Pictorial Bible Dictionary

TIED THE KNOT - *Marriage*

No relationship on this side of heaven will ever be enough.
Jack Deere

Pornography: The archenemy of fidelity.
Zow

Presented opportunities give way to prove with actions
the quality and genuineness of your words.
Zow

Responsibility is the ability to respond to every situation with
moral, legal, and mental acceptability.

Sex outside of God's ordained covenant is perversion.

Silence is expensive.
T.L. Hoff

Success is not final; failure is not fatal; it is the courage to continue that counts.
Winston Churchill

Thank you, Lord, for being patient with me,
for it is so hard to see when my eyes are on me.
Keith Green

Thankfulness thrives in a culture of trust.

That the woman was made from the side of Adam;
not made out of his head to rule over him,
nor out of his feet to be trampled by him,
but out of his side to be equal with him,
under his arm to be protected,
and near his heart to be beloved.
Matthew Henry

The Bible opens and closes with a wedding.

The biggest room in the house is the room for improvement.
Helmut Schmidt

The essence of womanhood is vulnerability.
Zow

The most important thing a father can do for his children is to love their mother.
Henry Ward Beecher, 1813-1887

The power of agreement with God's perfect will is increased in marriage.
Zow

The success or failure of all cultures bears greatly upon the
honor of God's design for marriage between one man and one woman.
Zow

TIED THE KNOT - *Marriage*

There ain't anything sexier than a righteous man!
Zow

There is no greater closeness than sharing one life.

We most experience loneliness when we:
Try to fix the past and control the future.
Want to get things perfect.
Blame others.
Focus on shame within.

Well married, a person has wings; poorly married, shackles.
Henry Ward Beecher

Who rules above you?
Zow

*WHOEVER DIGS A PIT WILL FALL INTO IT,
AND HE WHO ROLLS A STONE WILL HAVE IT ROLL BACK ON HIM.*
Proverbs 26:27

Twu Wuv!

I love your soul more than I love your friendship.

Zow

14
TENSILE STRENGTH
Relationships

TENSILE STRENGTH - Relationships

A woman's heart should be so close to God that a man should have to chase Him to find her.
C.S. Lewis

Accentuate the positive; eliminate the negative;
latch on to the affirmative; and don't mess with Mr. In-between.
Johnny Mercer and the Pied Pipers, 1945

Be what it is you want to attract.
Schatzie

Beware, Oh earth, the prophet who claims to know the time but never wears a watch.
Calvin Miller

Boundaries without consequences are mere suggestions.
Zow

Caution is needed in transparency. Only believers who have undergone victory
with Christ's blood, who walk in present faithfulness, are worthy of your heart's share.
Marilee Buckowski

Christians, sadly, set up their firing squads in circles.
Savado

Conflict is the price we pay for deeper intimacy.
Les Parrott

CONTEND, O LORD, WITH THOSE WHO CONTEND WITH ME;
FIGHT AGAINST THOSE WHO FIGHT AGAINST ME.
Psalm 35:1

DO NOT BE OVERCOME BY EVIL, BUT OVERCOME EVIL WITH GOOD.
Romans 12:21

...DO NOT SIT WITH WORTHLESS MEN,
NOR WILL I GO WITH PRETENDERS.
Psalm 26:4 NASB

Does your community even know you?

DO NOT TAKE SERIOUSLY ALL THE WORDS WHICH ARE SPOKEN,
LEST YOU HEAR YOUR SERVANT CURSING YOU.
FOR YOU ALSO HAVE REALIZED THAT YOU LIKEWISE
HAVE MANY TIMES CURSED OTHERS.
Ecclesiastes 7:21-22 NASB

Don't talk about situations, talk about Jesus.
God to Zow

Exit sign leaving church parking lot: "You are now entering the mission field."

Good is better than evil because it gets you in less trouble!

TENSILE STRENGTH - Relationships

Favor with God is given; favor with man is earned.

Great spirits have always encountered violent opposition from mediocre minds.
Albert Einstein

Happy people enjoy the scenery on a detour.
Gregory Benford

He makes a foe who makes a jest.
Benjamin Franklin

Honor is expressed through performance of positive acts;
reverence through the avoidance of negative ones.

I am most conceited when I'm trying to be humble.
Bob Marvos

I love your soul more than I love your friendship.
Zow

I know I am valuable to you when I do not have to perform and conform.

I would not regret it if the present generation behaves
worthy of the blessing you are laboring to secure for them.
Abigail Adams

If I need from others, they can control me.
God, alone, is the only Person worthy of this honor.

If you are not your brother's keeper, are you your brother's killer?
Zow

In plurality, joy is multiplied, pain is shared, and our backs are watched.

Is the fruit of my heart making others healthy or sick?

It is a known fact that birds confined in cages have a hard time producing.

It is not every question that deserves an answer.
Publius

It may be a drop in the ocean, but the ocean is made up of drops.
Mother Teresa

Just because a message isn't received doesn't mean it's not worth giving.

Know no man after the flesh but by the Spirit. This includes me!

Laudable efforts to restrict speech can become a
tool to silence critics or oppress minorities.
Barack Obama

LET US PURSUE THE THINGS WHICH MAKE FOR PEACE AND
THE THINGS BY WHICH ONE MAY EDIFY ANOTHER.
Romans 14:19

LET YOUR WORD BE 'YES, YES' OR 'NO, NO';
ANYTHING MORE THAN THIS COMES FROM THE EVIL ONE.
Matthew 5:37 NRSV

LOVE YOUR NEIGHBOR AS YOURSELF.
Jesus

Lower the volume, strengthen the argument.
Oren Yotom

Massive love allows and honors choice so much
that it may risk losing the relationship.
Zow

Measure your life in seasons of love.

Never add the weight of your character to a
charge against a person without knowing it to be true.
Abraham Lincoln

No cut downs.

Our priority should be to deal with the message, not the messenger.
Rowan Atkisson

R.E.S.T: Relinquishing External Solutions in Trials.

Sarcasm always separates to elevate.

Stand with anybody that stands right.
Stand with him while he is right and part with him when he goes wrong.
Abraham Lincoln

Ten men who speak make more noise than 10,000 who are silent.
Napoleon Bonaparte

Thankfulness makes you unoffendable.

The function of freedom is to free someone else.
Toni Morrison

TENSILE STRENGTH - Relationships

The gospel is not a formula.
It's not about what you say but from what place you are saying it.
Ana Mendez

The greatest punishment you have in this life is to always have it your way.

The price of greatness is responsibility.
Winston Churchill

The strongest weapon against hateful speech is not repression, but it is more speech.
Rowan Atkisson

The word of our testimony is the Word of God lived through us.

There is absolutely no defense to His love.

Those who dance are thought mad by those who do not hear the music.

To be seen is to be heard. What is my life saying?
Zow

Value every moment...God's life in me and in others.
Zow

We cannot genuinely love someone if at the same time
we demand something from them to spend upon ourselves.

WHAT IS DESIRED IN A MAN IS KINDNESS.
Proverbs 19:22

What you focus on the most is what you will release.

When I "nailed" His truth, did I "crucify" His love?

When you are offended you are setting yourself up for deception.
John Hammer

...WHO IS MY MOTHER AND WHO ARE MY BROTHERS?
Matthew 12:48

WOE TO YOU WHEN ALL SPEAK WELL OF YOU...
Luke 6:26a

You can't really say "yes" until you've learned to say "no."

You must be free of man's opinions to help man.
Joseph Prince

You were not made to fit in, you were made to stand out.
Set yourself apart from this corrupt generation.
Jim Caviezel

You will find as you look back upon your life that the moments when you have really lived,
are the moments when you have done things in the spirit of love.
Henry Drummond

Youth is the proper season for observation and attention.
Remember, an honest man is the noblest work of God.
Abigail Adams to son, John Quincy Adams

Love ya, man!

> *Watch for forked tongues and double-edged swords;*
> *they use the same words.*
>
> *Zow*

15
HANG LOOSE
Other Aware

A PERVERSE MAN SOWS STRIFE,
AND A WHISPERER SEPARATES THE BEST OF FRIENDS.
Proverbs 16:28

A person's name is the sweetest.
Dale Carnegie

A strong light offends weak eyes.

An error does not become a mistake until you refuse to correct it.

Ask a stranger, "What is it you inspire in others?"
Zow

Better to be hated for who you are than loved for who you are not.
Andre Gide

Careful listening to a person is the greatest compliment we can give him.
Dale Carnegie

Dissimulation: To hide under a false appearance.
Concealment of one's thoughts, feelings, or character pretense.
The inclination or practice of misleading others through lies or trickery.
Feigning. Hypocrisy. The act of concealing truth.

Do I walk in a room and say, "Here I am",
or do I walk in a room and say, "Here you are"?
Sally Reep

Don't try to unscrew the inscrutable.
Shared by O.T McRee

Envy is the ulcer of the soul.
Socrates

Expecting the world to treat you fairly because you are a good person
is like expecting a bull not to charge you because you are a vegetarian.
Rabbi Harold Kushner

First you care, then you give, then you love.

*HE WHO GIVES TO THE POOR WILL NEVER WANT,
BUT HE WHO SHUTS HIS EYES WILL HAVE MANY CURSES.*
Proverbs 28:27 NASB

*HE THAT GOES ABOUT AS A SLANDERER REVEALS SECRETS;
THEREFORE DO NOT ASSOCIATE WITH ONE WHO
FLATTERS WITH HIS LIPS.*
Proverbs 20:19

HE WHO WATERS OTHERS WILL HIMSELF BE REFRESHED.
Proverbs 11:25

How wonderful it is that nobody needs to wait a single moment
before starting to improve their world.
Anne Frank

If a man has a very decided character, and has a strongly accentuated career,
it is normally the case of course that he makes ardent friends and bitter enemies.
Theodore Roosevelt

If ever there exists a break in relationship with God, others, or even me,
there's a root of sin that needs to be confessed.

If you want a different result than what you are getting,
you need to do something different.

Improve yourself by other men's writings so that you shall come easily
by what others have labored hard for.
Socrates

In every encounter, we either give life or we drain it
Brennan Manning

Intimacy: IN – TO – ME – SEE

Just as theft of money exists, so does the theft of time.
Rabbi Moshe Luzzatto

Loose lips sink ships.

MAKE NO FRIENDSHIP WITH AN ANGRY MAN,
AND WITH A FURIOUS MAN DO NOT GO,
LEST YOU LEARN HIS WAYS
AND SET A SNARE FOR YOUR SOUL.
Proverbs 22:24-25

Much more depends on little things than is commonly imagined.
John Adams

No man indulges an error of judgment without sooner or later tolerating an error in practice.
Charles Spurgeon

Offenses dim the soul of the spirit's brightness.
Zow

People admire bold actions they consider courageous.

Sin never exists in a vacuum. It always affects others.
Schatzie

Strong minds discuss ideas; average minds discuss events;
weak minds discuss people.
Socrates

Test your opinions.

THERE ARE SIX THINGS THE LORD HATES,
YES, SEVEN THAT ARE AN ABOMINATION TO HIM:
A PROUD LOOK; A LYING TONGUE;
HANDS THAT SHED INNOCENT BLOOD;
A HEART THAT DEVISES WICKED PLANS;
FEET THAT ARE SWIFT IN RUNNING TO EVIL;
A FALSE WITNESS WHO SPEAKS LIES;
AND ONE WHO SOWS DISCORD AMONG BRETHREN.
Proverbs 6:16-19

There is a destiny that makes us brothers, none goes his way alone,
all that we send into the lives of others comes back into our own.
Edwin Markham

Those who broke my heart were just northern stars who pointed me straight to You.
Rascal Flatts

Unsolicited help or counsel is commonly perceived as control.
Zow

Walls are people's fears.

Watch for forked tongues and double-edged swords, they use the same words.
Zow

Watch for people who have the words, but don't sing the music.

Watch people's feet, not their mouths.

When I hide, I'm saying, "I want to be perfect; I want to belong;
I want to be significant".

When I hurl anger and accusation, I am saying,
"I want you to be perfect; I want you to make me OK;
I want you to give me a sense of belonging and significance".

When the debate is lost, slander becomes the tool of the loser.

*WHEN THERE ARE MANY WORDS, TRANSGRESSION AND OFFENSE ARE UNAVOIDABLE,
BUT HE WHO CONTROLS HIS LIPS AND KEEPS THOUGHTFUL SILENCE IS WISE.*
Proverbs 10:19 AMP

When we give an opportunity to give, people are more apt to feel safe.

Whenever one's decision rests upon an excuse, he enters deception.
Consequently, his decision is based upon a lie.
Sally Reep

WHOEVER DIGS A PIT WILL FALL INTO IT AND
HE WHO ROLLS A STONE WILL HAVE IT ROLL BACK ON HIM.
Proverbs 26:27

WITH THE SAME MEASURE YOU USE IT WILL BE MEASURED BACK TO YOU.
Matthew 7:2

You cannot accept another's incompleteness until you can accept your own.
Ted Roberts

You can't get blood from a stone.
Vicesimus Knox

You have nothing to prove in the kingdom of love, for love abounds to all.

You must choose not to be seduced.

 You first!

Follow the man as the man follows Me.

Depart from the man where the man departs from Me.

Zow

16
KNOT-A-FRAYED
Leadership

A chicken begets a chicken. A lion begets a lion.

A leader is a dealer of hope.
Napoleon

A leader who is weak in biblical principles will become prey to trends and spiritual fads.
Frank Damazio

A picture is worth a thousand words; an example is worth a thousand pictures.

A test of leadership is how you restore someone.

An entrepreneur moves himself. A catalyst moves others with him.

An individual who unselfishly tries to serve others has a tremendous advantage.
Dale Carnegie

Any jackass can kick a barn down,
but it requires a skilled carpenter to build one.
Rick Joyner

Anyone who has never made a mistake has never tried anything new.
Albert Einstein

Be brave now and the future will cherish your memory and praise your name.

...BE WISE AS SERPENTS AND HARMLESS AS DOVES.
Mark 10:16

Big dogs don't do anything small.

Casualness leads to casualties.
Jim Rohn

Change is not a destiny just as hope is not a strategy.
Rudy Giuliani

Children may close their ears to advice, but they open their eyes to examples.

"COME, FOLLOW ME",
JESUS SAID,
"AND I WILL MAKE YOU FISHERS OF MEN".
Matthew 4:19 BSB

Conformity: Painfully serving boring people since the beginning of time.

Constructive change offers the best method of avoiding destructive change.
Theodore Roosevelt

Difficulties are just things to overcome after all.
Ernest Shackleton

Difficulties show what men are. Therefore, when difficulties fall upon you,
remember that God, like a trainer of wrestlers,
has matched you with a rough young man.
Why? So, you may become an Olympic conqueror;
but it is not accomplished without sweat.
Epictetus

Do what you say!

Fear the Lord, lest you pervert justice.

Follow the man as the man follows Me.
Depart from the man where the man departs from Me.
God to Zow

Great hopes make great men.

Great leaders are great lovers. Great lovers are servants.

HE THAT KEEPS A ROYAL COMMAND
EXPERIENCES NO TROUBLE,
FOR A WISE HEART KNOWS THE PROPER TIME AND PROCEDURE.
Ecclesiastes 8:5

HE THAT RULES OVER MEN MUST BE JUST, RULING IN THE FEAR OF GOD.
HE WILL BE AS THE LIGHT OF THE MORNING WHEN THE SUN RISES,
EVEN AS THE MORNING WITHOUT CLOUDS,
AS THE TENDER GRASS SPRINGING OUT OF THE EARTH
BY CLEAR SHINING AFTER THE RAIN.
Samuel 23:3

HE WHO IS SLOW TO ANGER IS BETTER THAN HE WHO IS MIGHTY
AND HE WHO RULES HIS SPIRIT THAN HE WHO CAPTURES A CITY.
Proverbs 16:32

I hope you dance.

I wish I was the person my dog thinks I am.

If I were given a platform upon which to speak,
would people encounter me or the Lord Jesus?
Zow

If you do what you've always done, you'll get what you've always gotten.
If you linger on the outskirts, you will not speak in the gates.
God for Zow

It is difficulties that reveal the metal in the man.

It is not that I am so smart, but I stay with the questions much longer.
Albert Einstein

Just because a message isn't received doesn't mean it's not worth giving.
Segak

Know Risk! Know Reward!

Men do not judge us by our intentions, but by our acts.

Men who have a real call are not afraid of apprenticeships.
John G Lake

Much more depends on the little things than is commonly imagined.
John Adams

Old ceilings become new floors.

Ordinary men cease to be ordinary
when they not only ask such questions
but exert themselves to find the answers.
Benjamin Franklin

Pay attention to what you are reaping right now.
Are you eating good fruit or are you reaping weeds of futility?
Beware your seed.

People can't teach what they don't know;
people can't impart what they don't have;
and people can't lead where they won't go.

People function as either reflectors or shadows.

Possessions block our vision.
Mother Teresa

Premature responsibility breeds superficiality.
Albert Einstein

Rank does not confer privileges or give power; rather, it imposes responsibility.
Louis Armstrong

See one. Do one. Teach one.

The enemy thrives on capitalizing upon emotion to magnify a situation.
Zow

The first lesson, the cornerstone – OBEY!
A man may obey with that sullen contempt that is
worse than disobeying.
Harold Holzer, Dear Mr. Lincoln

The nobility of their mission will determine an army's resolve,
how well they are prepared for their mission,
and how well they are led.

The pessimist complains about the wind;
the optimist expects it to change;
the realist adjusts his sails.
William A. Ward

The questions are always more important than the answers.
Ernest Shackleton

The test of an individual's greatness is: What did he leave to grow?
Did he start men to think along fresh lines with a vigor that persisted after him?
By this test, Jesus stands first.
H. G. Wells

*THE WISE MAN LOOKS AHEAD. THE FOOL ATTEMPTS
TO FOOL HIMSELF AND WON'T FACE FACTS.
Proverbs 14:8 TLB*

There is no good following a man. You must follow a principle.
Lady Astor

Those who cannot remember the past are condemned to repeat it.
George Santayana

To create a change, we must change something.

To whom can I say, "Imitate me as I imitate Christ"?

Valor is the contempt of death and pain.
Tacitus

We are masters of the unsaid words, but slaves to those we let slip out.
Winston Churchill

We love most those leaders we would love to be like.
We rule by power or we rule by authority.

Well done is better than well said.
Benjamin Franklin

Whatever you are, be a good one.
Abraham Lincoln

When it was distributing food rations in Cambodia,
hundreds of people waited quietly for their share,
but when the fishnets were handed out, the crowds cheered!
Joseph Short, Executive Director of Oxram America

When we see the truth and reject the truth,
it strengthens our hearts in deception.

Without debate,
without criticism,
no administration and country can succeed, and
no republic can survive.
John F. Kennedy

You cannot fail unless you quit.
Abraham Lincoln

Don't just follow any bunny!

Aging: Reaping the mockings and moorings of my youth.

Zow

17
KNOTS OF OLD
Elders

KNOTS OF OLD - Elders

A group of tourists visiting a picturesque village
walked by an old man sitting beside a fence.
In a rather patronizing way, one tourist asked,
"Were any great men born in this village?"
The old man replied, "Nope, only babies!"
Leonard Ravenhill

A man is not meant to understand life, he is meant to live it.

After the game, the king and the pawn go into the same box.
Italian Proverb

Aging: Reaping the mockings and moorings of my youth.
Zow

Don't tell me about your father, show me your sons.

Even when they teach, men learn.
Seneca, 4 BC-65 A.D.

Experience is not what happens to you, but what you do with what happens to you.
Aldous Huxley

For your tomorrow we gave our today.
World War II Monument, Japan

Good judgment comes from experience...
and experience, well, that comes from poor judgment.
Mark Twain

Goodness matters more than intellect.

*HEAR ME... YOU WHO HAVE BEEN BURDENING ME
FROM BIRTH AND HAVE BEEN CARRIED FROM THE WOMB...*
Isaiah 46:3 LSB

Hindsight alone is not wisdom, and second-guessing is not strategy.
George W. Bush

Honor is expressed through the performance of positive acts;
reverence through the avoidance of negative ones.

Hope flies beyond the coming suffering.

*HUMILITY AND REVERENCE FOR THE LORD
WILL MAKE YOU BOTH WISE AND HONORED.*
Proverbs 15:33

If I have a pulse, I have a purpose.
Rich Wilkerson, Jr.

If there's a defining characteristic of a man as opposed to a boy, it is patience.
Lance Armstrong

IN THE MULTITUDE OF COUNSELORS THERE IS SAFETY.
Proverbs 11:14b

LISTEN TO YOUR FATHER, WHO GAVE YOU LIFE,
AND DO NOT DESPISE YOUR MOTHER WHEN SHE IS OLD.
Proverbs 23:22 NIV

NEVER SPEAK HARSHLY TO AN OLDER MAN, BUT APPEAL TO HIM RESPECTFULLY
AS YOU WOULD YOUR OWN FATHER.
Timothy 5:1-3

ONE GENERATION SHALL PRAISE YOUR WORKS TO ANOTHER,
AND SHALL DECLARE YOUR MIGHTY ACTS.
Psalm 145:4

Regard the honor and moral character of the man more than all other circumstances.
John Adams to Daughter, Nabby

Show me Your face, Lord, Your power and grace.
I can make it to the end if I can just see Your face.
Don Potter

The best index to a person's character is how he
treats people who can't do him any good and
how he treats people who can't fight back.
Abigail Van Buren

The early Church was married to poverty, prisons, and persecutions.
Today, the Church is married to prosperity, personality, and popularity.
Leonard Ravenhill

...THE FEAR OF THE LORD, THAT IS WISDOM,
AND TO DEPART FROM EVIL IS UNDERSTANDING.
Job 28:28

There should be priests to remind men that they will one day die.
It is necessary to have another kind of priest, called a poet,
To remind men that they are not yet dead.
G. K. Chesterton

We are born looking like our parents, but we end up looking like our choices.

When an old man dies, a library burns to the ground.
African Proverb

WHY DO YOU TRANSGRESS THE COMMANDMENT OF GOD
WHO IS THIS COMING UP FROM THE WILDERNESS,
LEANING UPON HER BELOVED?
Song of Solomon 8:5

WISDOM IS FOUND WITH THE ELDERLY,
AND UNDERSTANDING COMES WITH LONG LIFE.
Job 12:12 BSB

You cannot receive from what you don't honor.

"You must be frank in the world. Frankness is the child of honesty and courage.
Say just what you mean to do on every occasion. Never do anything wrong to make a friend
or to keep one. The man who requires you to do so is purchased at a sacrifice. Deal kindly but
firmly with all your classmates. You will find it the policy that wears the best.
Above all, do not appear to others what you are not."
Robert Lee, to his son Robert Lee Jr., 1860

YOU SHALL RISE BEFORE THE GRAY HEADED AND
HONOR THE PRESENCE OF AN OLD MAN, AND
FEAR YOUR GOD, I AM THE LORD.
Leviticus 19:32

YOUR CARE FOR OTHERS IS THE MEASURE OF YOUR GREATNESS.
Luke 9:48

Youth is the gift of nature, but age is a work of art.
David Mamet

Youth is wasted on the young.
George Bernard Shaw

Sakes, already?!

> There are no excuses where there is a cross.
>
> Zow

18
END OF THE ROPE

Next Stop, Eternity!

A life unexamined is not worth living.
Plato, 428-348 BC

A man is what he is, not what he used to be.

A white soldier asked a group of slaves after struggling nine days through a swamp
what sustained them during the terrible ordeal.
One replied,
"I saw a lamp of life ahead and the lamp of death behind."
Harriet Tubman

*ALL THE DAYS OF MY WARFARE WOULD I WAIT,
UNTIL MY RELEASE SHOULD COME.*
Job 14:14 WEB

An investment in knowledge pays the best interest.
Benjamin Franklin

AND IT IS APPOINTED FOR MEN TO DIE ONCE, BUT AFTER THIS THE JUDGMENT.
Hebrews 9:27

*AND THIS IS ETERNAL LIFE, THAT THEY MAY KNOW YOU, THE ONLY TRUE GOD,
AND JESUS CHRIST WHOM YOU HAVE SENT.*
John 17:3

Are you living too much for time and not wholly for eternity?

Aspice, venturo laetentur ut omnia:
Look! See how they are full of joy at the age to come.
Virgil

Cartoon: Satan greeting people at the gates of hell...
"You'll find there is no right and wrong here, just what works for you."
Lee B. Strobel, The Case for Christ

Come as you are; leave as He is.

Die like a hero going home.
Chief Tecumseh

*DO NOT LOVE THE WORLD OR THE THINGS OF THE WORLD...
FOR ALL THAT IS IN THE WORLD, THE LUST OF THE FLESH,
THE LUST OF THE EYES, AND THE PRIDE OF LIFE,
IS NOT OF THE FATHER, BUT IS OF THE WORLD.
AND THE WORLD IS PASSING AWAY, AND THE LUST OF IT;
BUT HE WHO DOES THE WILL OF GOD ABIDES FOREVER.*
1 John 2:15-17

Do not settle for a false finish line.

Eternity starts now.
Schatzie

Faith sees through to the promises of God;
faithlessness sees only in reverse.
Zow

Finish your assignment in FAITH!

FOR IT IS APPOINTED FOR MEN TO DIE ONCE, BUT AFTER THIS THE JUDGMENT.
Hebrews 9:27

GOD HAS PUT ETERNITY INTO MEN'S HEARTS.
Ecclesiastes 3:11

Hell, it is said, is truth realized too late.
Thomas Hobbes

Hell wasn't intended for people. But for those that want a place that has nothing to do with God, the gift is theirs.
Zow

I am your beginning and your end.
If it doesn't start with Me, it will not end with Me.
God to Zow

I have only one life and it is short enough.
Why waste it on the things I don't want the most?

*I HEARD A VOICE FROM HEAVEN SAYING TO ME,
"WRITE: BLESSED ARE THE DEAD WHO DIE IN THE LORD FROM NOW ON'."
"YES," SAYS THE SPIRIT,
"THAT THEY MAY REST FROM THEIR LABORS,
AND THEIR WORKS FOLLOW THEM."
Revelation 14:13-14*

I would rather people hate me with the knowledge that I tried to save them.
Keith Green

If I have seen further, it is by standing on the shoulder of giants.
Isaac Newton

If sinners are damned, at least let them leap to hell over our dead bodies.
And if they perish, let them perish with our arms wrapped around their knees.
Charles Spurgeon

If something is visible, it is temporary; if it is invisible, it is eternal.

If the President of your own country won't allow you into
the White House just because you are an American citizen,
why would the Lord of heaven and earth allow you into His home in heaven
simply because you are a faithful church member?

If you get where you are going, where will you be?
If you get what you want, what will you have?

If your riches are yours, why don't you take them with you to the other world?
Poor Richard's Almanac

Is what you're doing now worth Christ's death?
It is God's perception of an event that should shape me, not the event itself.
Zow

...IT IS THE ONE WHO HAS ENDURED TO THE END WHO WILL BE SAVED.
Matthew 10:22 NASB

It's the difference between seeing a hole in the wall and looking through it.

Joy is not where you have been; joy is Who is waiting for you at the end.
Petra

Life consists of taken opportunities and missed opportunities.
Life is lived forward but understood backward.
Soren Kierkegaard

Life is short; Death is sure. Sin the cause; Christ the cure.

Never offer the eternal on the altar of the temporary.

Severe trouble in a true believer has the effect of loosening the roots
of his soul earthward and tightening the anchor of his heart heavenward.
Charles Spurgeon

THE FOOL HAS SAID IN HIS HEART, "THERE IS NO GOD."
THEY ARE CORRUPT, THEY HAVE DONE ABOMINABLE WORKS,
THERE IS NONE WHO DOES GOOD.
Psalm 14:1

The road to hell is paved with good intentions.
St. Bernard of Clairvaux, 1090-1153

The safest road to hell is the gradual one, the gentle slope:
soft underfoot, without sudden turnings, without milestones, without signposts.
C. S. Lewis

THE STING OF DEATH IS SIN, AND THE STRENGTH OF SIN IS THE LAW.
BUT THANKS BE TO GOD,
WHO GIVES US VICTORY THROUGH OUR LORD JESUS CHRIST.
1 Corinthians 15:56

THE WAY OF LIFE WINDS UPWARD FOR THE WISE,
THAT HE MAY TURN AWAY FROM HELL BELOW.
Proverbs 15:24

There is perhaps nothing worse than reaching the top of the ladder and
discovering that you're on the wrong wall.
Joseph Campbell

To hell with the devil. To heaven with the people.

We more readily put off immediate fulfillment when we
understand there are eternal implications.

What will my active life message do to someone who has two weeks to live?

When it's all been said and done, all my treasures will be as nothing.
Only what I've done for love's reward will stand the test of time.
Robin Mark

When Satan reminds you of your past, remind him of his future.

When the trumpet blows, we will GO!

When will your heart decide?
Disney

You ARE going to die. Does this surprise you?
Prepare as if your life depends upon it!
Zow

You may escape taxes, but you will never escape eternity.

You shook the Lion's paw...you're free!
Harriet Tubman

Your future appears to be in full bloom!

KNOT THE END...

HONORING MY STRONG THREADS

HE WHO PURSUES RIGHTEOUSNESS AND MERCY FINDS LIFE, RIGHTEOUSNESS, AND HONOR.
Proverbs 21:21

These, my finest threads, are forever woven into my rope!
You will find the longest threads listed first. Their favorite quotes reveal them.
Their influence upon me is boundless.
"These are the excellent ones in whom is all my delight".
Zow

MOM / "SCHATZIE"
Unto God be true!

RUTH ANN SCHULTZ
People live by the love for them that is in the hearts of other people.
Tolstoy

DONNA JOHNSON
If at first, you don't succeed, try, try again.

BRIAN KOLZOW
It's good enough for who it's for.
B. Kolzow

KATHRYN STEVENS
A careless word may kindle strife; A cruel word may wreck a life.
A bitter word may hate instill; A brutal word may smite and kill.
A gracious word will smooth the way; A joyous word will lift the day;
A timely word will lessen stress; A loving word will heal and bless.
Anon.

CAROLYN SUCCOP
We are rich, for He was poor; is this not a wonder?
Therefore, praise Him evermore, on this earth and yonder!
Urban Langhans

ANGIE HOBSON
Courage doesn't always roar. Sometimes it is a quiet voice that says, "I will try again tomorrow."

MIKE BAIRD
Give yourself to something, and it will give back to you.

"KD" HOLT
The grass isn't greener on the other side; it's greener where you water it.
Shared by Ted Roberts

NOEL LESH
Humility is not thinking less about yourself; it is thinking about yourself less.
C.S. Lewis

JAMIE SAGERSER
' Course He isn't safe. But He's good. He's the King, I tell you!
C.S. Lewis

JU JU KING
Listening to God is essential to walking with God.

MARILYN HUME
And it came to pass.

DAN KING
God prepares great men for great tasks by great trials.
J.K. Gressett

TAMI HOFF
What you think about God is the most important thing about you.
A.W. Tozer "

CHELE "BABE" WOOD
If you live your life by following God, you will never be disappointed.

DEBBIE DUGGAN
Let your heart sing!
D. Duggan

ANNE NESBIT
What color is your light?

SALLY REEP
Always do the right thing, and it will take care of people.
If you take care of people first, you will always compromise the right thing.

SANDI ROBINSON
You will show me the path of life; in your presence is fullness of joy;
at your right hand there are pleasures forevermore.
Psalm 16:11

JAMES ROBINSON
Where the word of the King is, there is power.
Ecclesiastes 8:4

HONORING MY NEW THREADS

THOUGH ONE MAY BE OVERPOWERED
BY ANOTHER, TWO CAN WITHSTAND HIM.
A CORD OF THREE STRANDS IS NOT EASILY BROKEN.
Ecclesiastes 4:12

Enriched and strengthened by the workings of God in these lives,
I present my younger threads to you in their own quotes. My love goes deep!
He is the Lord of these beauties!
Zow

AARON DENSMORE
The measure of a man is not how many serve him but how many he serves.

ALLEY VALLOTTON
Joy and sorrow are friends too. Joy is not afraid of sorrow.
Rather, it embraces it because it knows joy will come again tomorrow.
Alley Vallotton

AURORA GRACIA
The greatest thing you'll ever learn is to love and be loved in return.

DESTINY KEIL
If it won't challenge you, it won't change you.

JESSICA RAE ELLIS
Scatter your flowers over the graves and walk away.
Be good-natured and untidy in your exuberance!

JESSICA WILMOT
The storms you can sleep through are the ones you have authority over.
Bill Johnson

KATIE SMITH
Who God is to you, He will be through you!

KELLIE SCHOENECKER
I have been crucified with Christ. It's no longer I who live but Christ who lives in me.
Galatians 2:20

LOGAN JONES
Whenever it's breezy, swing easy.
H.S. Golf Coach

MIRANDA MCROWLAND
Humility is the way forward.
Kris Vallotton

MELODY GEORGE
There are thousands striking at the branches of evil to the one who is striking at the root.
Henry David Thoreau

PARIS MARTIN
Raise your words, not your voice; It is rain that grows flowers, not thunder.
Rumi

DEREK and STACY HOYT
The enemy knows he MUST leave the moment we truly realize we belong to Jesus.
He's scared to death we are going to find that out!

STETSON WHEAT
Outside of God, even the most extraordinary can feel mundane.
When you let God fill your adventure, even the most mundane can feel extraordinary.
S. Wheat

TARYN CLAPP
You either live out of being overwhelmed, or you live out of your overflow with God.

"Schatzie"

GRANNY KNOT TRIBUTE

Anchored in grace, not her perfection.
Wonderfully loved by Spirit, she lives.
Facing her God, her sureness of wisdom,
She prays us all upwards and points us to Him!

Dearest Mom...

What God has threaded in my life through you will take eternity to disclose.
His reaches to mentor me in His ways have come through your wisdom and concerted diligence.
You taught me to know God through His own words and not religion.
Deeper still are my tears of gratitude –
for His love, through you, has threaded every meaningful relationship in my life.

You have been the mother many would dream of having, and few have known,
for we share the deep and eternal treasure of God's friendship.

Your sacrificial love, forgiving nature, discipline, and prophetic influence can never be repaid.
I will live to give thanks to God by extending this love to others.
There is no one in this life who means more to me!

This book started with you, was inspired by you, and so it is dedicated to you!

Thank you, Mama!
I love you, forever!

Yours,
"Elizabethakanezar"

 You can't push a rope!

ZOW'S BIO

Karen "Zow" Kolzow has postured her life toward this end: to know and to be loved by God, to love others, and to know wisdom. Trials and shipwrecks in her own life and others have been the tutors of her journey. As God has brought her wholeness and freedom, her hunger has grown to see a generation living out the design of their destiny in fullness of fellowship with Him. Zow has written *Knots in Aunty's Rope* to propel young and old forward in this hope.

As an inspirer of people, Zow mentors with the intent to encourage excellence, create community, and build up individuals to walk in robust faith. By creating beautiful environments, extending gracious hospitality, ministering through her piano and artwork, and sharing insights from history and study, Zow enriches those in her sphere of influence. Those connections are playfully enhanced by outdoor adventures, competitive and strategic board games, and anything to do with food and music. She and her yappie-poo call the Great Northwest "home".

Made in the USA
Las Vegas, NV
17 January 2024